PRAISE FOR *LOOK BOTH WAYS*

"Deserves a spot on every tuned-in woman's bookshelf."
—Cathi Hanauer, author of *Sweet Ruin* and
editor of *The Bitch in the House*

"*Feminista* supreme Jennifer Baumgardner traces the roots of her bi-sexuality and explores the ways in which it has informed her per-spective on politics, activism, writing, feminism, and the world at large . . . *Look Both Ways* is a sharp, entertaining read . . . It makes for a compelling analysis of what it means to be a woman who is neither straight nor gay, neither here nor there, but *both*."
—Laura Barcella, *Bust*

"Lively . . . A valentine to . . . the benefits of bisexuality for today's young women . . . At its dizzying best, it's an absorbing tale of how discovering her own bisexuality, at 23, changed Baumgard-ner's life." —Susan Comminos, *San Francisco Chronicle*

"There is no question about it, *Look Both Ways* . . . is going to spark the smoldering bisexual debate in the queer and straight commu-nities, launching a new generation of 'bifeminist' activists into a call to mobility and visibility." —Heather Cassell, *Bay Area Reporter*

"Baumgardner's voice remains as compelling as ever, not only be-cause she writes with the candor of your closest friend, but because she herself appears to be learning and questioning along with the reader." —Fiorella Valdesolo, *Nylon*

"A provocative heads-up." —Annie Wagner, *The Stranger*

"Baumgardner is generally thoughtful and honest, with a refresh-ing sense of humor about herself and her politics."
—Rebecca Tuhus-Dubrow, *Salon*

"Bisexuality . . . is not about sexual behavior; it's about engaging with the world in an inclusive, open way. Baumgardner shines at the center of this book as a titillating, thoughtful, and refreshingly earnest model of that kind of engagement."

—Courtney Martin, *Bitch*

"Baumgardner does a wise and witty job of figuring out the hidden messages and reading them to us in her deliciously cool and contemporary voice: the one that gives us hope for the feminist future."

—Vivian Gornick

"Reinventing the *personal is the political* narrative that's been the staple of feminist writing since the 1960s, [Baumgardner] documents an emerging sexual consciousness that builds on the feminist dream of a better world."

—*Tikkun*

"Educational and juicy."

—Beth Greenfield, *Time Out New York*

"Employing telling details from her own and others' experiences, Baumgardner consistently emphasizes the need for listening to women's stories rather than focusing on the gender of their sex partners . . . This significant contribution to sociosexual and gender studies helps build bridges from feminism to the gay rights movement."

—Whitney Scott, *Booklist*

"Baumgardner . . . makes plenty of astute observations about the intersection of bisexuality and feminism, particularly how bi women bring 'gay expectations' of equality, respect, and sexual fulfillment to their relationships with men."

—Ann Friedman, *Mother Jones*

JENNIFER BAUMGARDNER

LOOK BOTH WAYS

Jennifer Baumgardner, coauthor of *Manifesta* and *Grass-roots: A Field Guide for Feminist Activism*, is the creator of the I Had an Abortion project and producer of the film by that name. She frequently writes and lectures on feminism, activism, and popular culture for magazines and on college campuses around the country. She lives in Williamsburg, Brooklyn, with her son, Skuli.

ALSO BY JENNIFER BAUMGARDNER

Coauthored with Amy Richards

Manifesta: Young Women, Feminism, and the Future

Grassroots: A Field Guide for Feminist Activism

Series Editor: Feminist Classics

The Female Eunuch,
   by Germaine Greer

The Dialectic of Sex: The Case for Feminist Revolution,
   by Shulamith Firestone

Memoirs of an Ex–Prom Queen,
   by Alix Kates Shulman

LOOK BOTH WAYS

Bisexual Politics

LOOK BOTH WAYS

JENNIFER BAUMGARDNER

FARRAR, STRAUS AND GIROUX
New York

Farrar, Straus and Giroux
18 West 18th Street, New York 10011

The Library of Congress has cataloged the hardcover edition as follows:
Baumgardner, Jennifer, 1970–
    Look both ways : bisexual politics / by Jennifer Baumgardner. —1st ed.
      p.   cm.
    Includes index.
    ISBN-13: 978-0-374-19004-0 (hardcover : alk. paper)
    ISBN-10: 0-374-19004-6 (hardcover : alk. paper)
    1. Bisexual women. 2. Bisexual feminism. I. Title.

    HQ74.B38 2007
    306.76'50820973—dc22

                                               2006022178

Paperback ISBN-13: 978-0-374-53108-9
Paperback ISBN-10: 0-374-53108-0

Designed by Debbie Glasserman

www.fsgbooks.com

10 9 8 7 6 5 4 3 2 1

This book is dedicated to
the loves of my life (so far):
A.N.H., S.R.D., A.E.R., and G.F.S.

CONTENTS

CONTENTS

I had two breakups, two moves, a pregnancy, and (finally) an infant while writing this book. Thanks to the following people for taking care of me and my son, and for helping with the manuscript: my parents, David and Cynthia; Andrea Baumgardner; Jessica Baumgardner; Constance DeCherney; Amelia Freeman-Lynde; Anastasia Higgin-botham; Christine and Marianne Jensch; Elizabeth Maki; Ali Price; Amy Richards; Barbara Seaman; Gordon Smethurst; and Sara Jane Stoner. Thanks to the people above and to Lisa Johnson, Alix Kates Shulman, Hannah Wallace, and Naomi Weisstein for reading drafts.

I'm grateful to the many women who were interviewed or offered their stories for this book, especially Dolores Alexander, Jan Clausen, Meg Daly, Melissa Dessereau, Ani DiFranco, Liza Featherstone, Debbie Grossman, Laura Ko-gel, Alix Kates Shulman, and Gareth White.

Thanks to Denise Oswald, my editor at FSG, and to Jill Grinberg, my agent, for their continued advice, support, talent, and friendship.

LOOK BOTH WAYS

INTRODUCTION

INTRODUCTION

"We're all straight here, right?" I asked the five twenty- to twenty-two-year-olds in my charge when I was the newly minted internship coordinator at *Ms.* magazine, just before launching into some now-forgotten description of office politics. We were having half-price sushi after work. It was 1993.

"Yes."

"Yes."

"Yes."

"Yes."

"Um, pretty much."

The "pretty much" straight intern was named Anastasia. I don't remember what my point was, or why I needed to take a poll of their sexuality before I made my next comment, but in that second of not-quite-unanimous agreement, I flushed. I was exposed in what could have been called my heterosexism, but that's not what prompted the blood to rush to my cheeks—I was looking at the beautiful Anastasia with new eyes. "Pretty much, huh? *You?*" She seemed so . . . normal. I was just beginning to realize how hot the boyish and sexy lesbians in the office were to me but Anastasia was

something different. She was a former prom queen from
outside of Pittsburgh, a young Madonna Ciccone with large
breasts and mascara'd eyes, a girlie-girl. For the first time, I
took stock of her chunky black boots, her recently shorn
hair. *Pretty much straight?*

Months later, mid–love affair, we laughed hysterically
that I, her girlfriend, had opened a (usually politically correct) *Ms.* intern dinner by asking if we were "all straight
here." Who knew then that I was actually asking myself the
question: "Jen—all straight? Are you sure?"

I'm not all straight as it turns out. And I'm not all gay, either. Over the years, I have come to figure out where I stand
sexually—which is neither straight nor gay—and in the
process I've recognized how inherently problematic the
more common either/or viewpoint is. As a working frame-
work, I propose that sexuality itself can be thought of as a
combination of three identifying elements: It's whom you
sleep with (one's sexual practices), whom you set up a home
with (one's everyday life), and how you identify yourself
(one's labels). The "problem of bisexuality," as Freud refers
to it, is that being a mixture of straight and gay doesn't exist
in our imaginations even as we live bisexual lives in reality.
The common assertion is that so-called bisexuals aren't truly
attracted to both sexes but are actually straight but otherwise experimenting or are really gay but not able to own up.
In other words, it's a phase, and one that is generally disparaged at that.

This mind-set is typical. On July 5, 2005, *The New York
Times* published an article entitled "Straight, Gay or Lying?
Bisexuality Revisited," reporting on a study of 101 adult
men, 33 of whom identified as bisexual, 30 as heterosexual,
and 38 as gay. The researchers measured the men's responses to same-sex and heterosexual porn by "objective"
(penile sensors) and "subjective" (dials turned by the men to
indicate levels of heat) measures. They found that the bisex-

ual men did not experience an even distribution of arousal among gay and straight pornography. A scientist who wasn't part of the study, Dr. Lisa Diamond of the University of Utah, commented approvingly for the article: "Research on sexual orientation has been based almost entirely on self-reports, and this is one of the few good studies using physiological measures." The *Times*'s story summed up, quoting the researchers, that *"there is no hint that true bisexual arousal exists* [and] . . . *for men, arousal is orientation"* (italics are mine). Conclusion: In case you didn't get it from the headline, bisexuality is a state of mind, not a biological state of being. In other words, it's a fraud.

But underneath that public gloss is another story. When I read the actual study, it became clear that the reporter, as well as the researchers, were interpreting the data with a bias. In fact, their research showed that all males in the study were somewhat bisexual—all were at least slightly aroused by their stated non-preferred sex. The authors even come right out and say, "This suggests that most men may possess a certain capacity for bisexual arousal although the magnitude of the arousal is quite modest"—but this point is not quoted in the *Times* article. Among the bi-identified men, "subjective" arousal was quite high; it was only the "objective" arousal that was modest. Even these researchers would probably admit that sexuality comprises much more than the levels of blood rushing to one's genitals. Furthermore, how we interpret our arousal, modest or not, has much to do with the narrative of our lives. Fleeting feelings for the intern Anastasia might have played out differently had we met at *The New York Times* rather than *Ms*.

After declaring that bisexuality does not exist, the article tosses off the contradictory assertion that, in women, "bisexual arousal may indeed be the norm," with no accompanying article entitled "Women: You Say You're Gay or Straight? You're Obviously Lying!" The aforementioned Dr.

Diamond's own research of ninety women, half of whom identified as lesbian, yielded the result that most had had relationships with both men and women. So perhaps Anastasia and I, being ladies, might have clicked anywhere. In the week following the publication of "Straight, Gay or Lying," it was the number one most e-mailed article. Given how few, if any, supposed bisexuals there are, I was surprised by the interest.

Such clear bias in a clinical study should be shocking, but it's not so much when you consider that those scientists were just voicing what most people already think. Take, for example, how the character Phoebe Buffay on *Friends* explains looking both ways in a song she wrote for children: "sometimes men love women / sometimes men love men / and then there are bisexuals / though some just say they're kidding themselves / Lalalala lalala . . ." Less colorfully, Elizabeth Wurtzel put it to me like this: "You have to choose eventually, right?"

On the contrary. What I'm asserting is that we are looking at bisexuality the wrong way, making the identity entirely dependent on someone other than the bisexual person him- or herself. If I'm dating a man, I'm straight. If I'm dating a woman, I'm a lesbian. But sexuality is not who you sleep with, it's who you are. It doesn't change according to who is standing next to you.

Ever since realizing that I wasn't all straight, I have opened my eyes to the hordes of other women who aren't quite straight either. As Margaret Atwood has described the Canadian citizen in the United States: we walk among you; you don't even know we are different. (*You* being the straight and the gay.) But nobody knows much about us "pretty much" types because, well, the lives of bisexual women? What a tedious, irrelevant topic! At least that is what I've gathered from my failure to place articles about this issue throughout my writing career. In 1995, while I was at *Ms.*, I penned an essay on bisexuality and younger feminists. Though it had been assigned to me, the magazine never came close to running it. In fact, the editorial meeting in which we discussed my draft left me with the distinct sense that I had nothing to say on the matter, and that there wasn't much anyone else could say about it either. "You seem confused," one helpful editor said, looking at me with concern. "You need to think about it more." I had just begun writing professionally and still filtered many of my ideas through a lens labeled "What I Think *Ms.* Wants to Hear," so I'm sure that the draft did leave much to be desired, though its improvement was supposed to happen in the editing process. I took the editors' lukewarm response as a sure sign that bisexuality and I weren't ready for prime time, and put the draft away.

A year or so later, after I had written long stories on other topics for *Jane, Playboy, Glamour,* and *The Nation,* an editor at *Details* took me out to lunch to discuss story ideas. Feeling more confident about my prose and my instincts, I trotted out the idea of writing about the growing phenomenon of straight-seeming women of my generation—the ones raised after *Roe* and Title IX—having girlfriends, a situation that those raised in the fifties probably wouldn't have risked. "Hmmm," said the very smart, very pregnant, very married editor. "Isn't that something people outgrow? I mean, it's pretty hard to sustain for life. Besides, I certainly can't see a whole article on bisexuality." I detected a whiff of nostalgia in her tone, but no assignment.

At another lunch, this time with an elegant editor at a women's magazine, I suggested my doing a feature on the widespread occurrence of girls having affairs with girls, and its implications. She replied, "I don't think that would fly for us; 99.5 percent of our readers are just straight." *Right,* I thought, *just like 99.5 percent of priests, the army, and the Boy Scouts.*

I did manage to write a half-page definition of bisexuality

for a book on "over-the-counter culture." A scintillating
sample of the edited entry: "sexual non-preference of the
'90s for those who take romantic or sexual partners regardless of gender." Still, I couldn't persuade the editors of that
book to include an entire essay on "straight" women who
fall in love with other women, despite my belief that it was
a legitimate phenomenon. In perhaps a weak moment, I included a bit about bisexuality in an article about my "slut
phase" for *Maxim*, the men's answer to *Cosmo*. In "horn-dog"
parlance (*Maxim's* signature style—in fact, they injected the
word *horn-dog* into the finished piece, lest anyone forget that
Maxim men are horn-dogs), I argued that my slut phase was
the time in my life when I took control of my sex life; no
longer waiting for men to ask me out, I chose whom I
wanted. My sexual empowerment, of course, was marked by
considerable rolling around in bed with women. My line
was, "These [people I was casually dating] weren't guys I
would bring home to Mom. In fact, they often weren't even
guys." But even when confined to one quick sentence, the
reference to bisexuality was cut from the final piece. The
editor said it just confused matters.

Didn't Helen Gurley Brown tell us that sex sells? In a sex-
obsessed world, it appeared that no one wanted to know
about bisexual sex. Why? Well, *because it's not a "real" sexual orientation somehow. Reading about it is confusing because bisexuals themselves are just confused. Besides it's just a phase. Did I mention that bi is
code for gay? And, you know, it's just a trendy way for straight girls to
fit in with other radical or oppressed folks.*

In the face of all of this denial and disdain, I noted that
the longest chapter in Nancy Friday's *My Secret Garden*, the
seventies book of female sex fantasies, is devoted to heterosexual women's fantasies about other women. *Straight* women.
Lesbian fantasies. *Longest* chapter. Then there are the ubiquitous straight girls kissing gay-ish girls on popular TV shows
such as *Buffy the Vampire Slayer*, Mischa Barton's bisexual

character on *The OC*, Claire's exploration of bisexuality on HBO's *Six Feet Under*. Even Samantha, the liberated older woman famed for loving well-endowed men on *Sex and the City*, got together with a lesbian (played by Sonia Braga). These female characters aren't always meant to be gay— although Willow on *Buffy* refers to herself as "gay now" and Samantha briefly declares herself a lesbian—but rather women who look both ways, seeking out men and women for their own sexual and emotional benefit. They appear to be straight *and* gay (or, at least, gay-ish). And, in being so, they both strengthen and complicate the concept of gay rights and feminism.

These subconscious and conscious images of bisexuality in ads, on TV, and in erotica reflect the lives of real women and girls—including me. It's something we see in the girls in their hiphuggers and strappy tank tops holding hands outside Ani DiFranco concerts. We see it in Catherine Wing, a Wellesley grad who told me she identifies as bisexual (going so far as to land an internship with the radically queer Audre Lorde Project in Brooklyn), even though she has never kissed a girl or had a girlfriend. It's in my high school classmate in Fargo who left her husband for a woman who played on the local softball team (natch!), and then remarried her husband after two years. A 2005 study by the Centers for Disease Control found that 11 percent of women ages fifteen to forty-four reported having had some form of sexual experience with women; women were also three times more likely than men to have had both male and female partners in the last year. The younger the woman, the more likely she'd had a same-sex encounter.[1] Over the past decade, I have come across hundreds of girls who have had significant experiences with other girls, and *not* simply in order to turn on their boyfriends. In fact, even the naysaying, mother-to-be *Details* editor ended up leaving her husband for a woman.

To understand women who look both ways requires hearing their stories, not just noting the sex of their current partner. And when you listen closely, it's apparent these women have learned something crucial in these relationships. For myself, I can say that having had relationships with both men and women has given me information on how to be more liberated with men, and less sexist with women.

Is it possible that this phase of rampant female bisexuality represents an evolution—is it the new *Sex and the Single Girl?* When Helen Gurley Brown told the story of single working women in her 1962 bestseller, she exposed the outrageous but key fact that these women engaged in a brand of sex that they weren't allowed to have: sex outside of marriage. She trumpeted the news that "good girls *do*, and they don't die from it."

Why did these girls, good and bad, have this illicit sex, these relationships that weren't girded to hearth and home? They wanted freedom and power and love and pleasure. Women had sexual relationships with people they wanted to learn from and with whom they felt a spark. They did it because it felt right, and why should they miss out? They did it to make the best relationship they could, and to learn what a good relationship was. Just as the women of Brown's generation began to regard single-girl sex as a good idea, girls today look both ways not because it's a phase and we're painfully trendy, or because we are pathological and weak, but because there is *plenty* in it for us.

If only I could be internship coordinator again. I'd have such good advice this time: *Look both ways, girls.*

CHAPTER 1

FIRST LOOK

She was aiming for something beyond the usual, because the usual denied her full humanity.

—Ann Powers, from her 1993 liner notes for the Janis Joplin box set

Who invented typical girls?

—The Slits, "Typical Girls"

If you're walking down the street in London, you'll find helpful words stenciled on the street at most crosswalks: LOOK RIGHT, reminds one, where the traffic whizzes by on the left side of the street. LOOK LEFT, instructs the next, as cars zoom past on the right. Sometimes you stand on a curb poised to take a step, look down, and the street tells you LOOK BOTH WAYS.

In 1993, I stood poised at an unfamiliar intersection of attraction, sex, and love—and I looked both ways. My world was New York City, and it looked like this:

Dinkins was mayor. No one walked down the street or sat at a café or drove their car while yakking on a cell phone. There were no Starbucks. I bought fifty-cent coffee from vendors stationed in aluminum carts. I hadn't heard of the Internet or the Web, and when I did, I took to using that early-nineties überterm, the *Infobahn* (a German spin on *information superhighway*—fortunately, both terms fell out of use). Dot-coms had yet to be invented, much less to inflate and then implode. E-mail was something that a few VAX geeks at my college used, but it had nothing to do with real life. Ellen was not out, and "outing" (the gay community's version of a suicide bombing) loomed as potential annihilation, terrorizing closeted homosexuals. Grunge was but a year or two old; Riot Grrls were writing each other love letters and starting bands. Kate Moss was causing a sensation with her waif look. *PC* meaning "politically correct" was as popular a term as *PC* meaning "personal computer." A rakish and idealistic Bill Clinton had just become president number forty-two, seemingly a victory for the politically correct, myself included. Doomed, intelligent Hillary was still being presented as a partner, not a First Lady, and the Clintons still believed that the nation would see that as a good thing. Bill's "Don't Stop Thinking About Tomorrow" idealism had retracted enough to squeeze out gays from the military. George Stephanopoulos was considered hot.

On January 10 of that year, at age twenty-two and half a year out of the safety of a small liberal arts college in the Midwest, I boarded a train in Fargo at 2:30 a.m. and, thirty-five hours and two Milan Kundera books later, arrived in Manhattan to start an internship at *Ms.* magazine. I carried just two suitcases and a Coach briefcase I would never use. What I didn't have was a paying job, a place to live, or friends—other than Michael Gardner, that is, a slightly older pal from my hometown who was fabulous, gay, and a dresser for the long-running Broadway phenomenon known as *Cats.* He had said I could stay with him and his boyfriend for a week until I found a room of my own. Michael had been instrumental in my deciding to move to New York; I had almost moved to Chicago. "Honey, *Chicago?*" Michael had said. "You need to be in New York. Why do NoDoz when there's crack available?"

In my mind, I had arrived simply by making New York City—Manhattan—my new address. You don't have to be from a small landlocked town with six months of winter to know that New York is one of *those* places—where mystique and myth and overpopulation and opportunity mix to create the frantic cocktail known as freedom. Growing up in Fargo, I had always feared that I was missing out on the party. My hopes for myself in the Midwest were grandiose, but they were often at odds with my earnest feminist proclivities. I wanted to be a fashion model, at least for catalogues; I would meet Bernadette Peters and become her understudy, or perhaps her personal assistant. Merely being in a place where the high rollers of those ambitions lived and worked and debauched and grocery shopped made me feel this close to a contract, a gig, a job, the glamorous life. A journal entry from January 19, 1993, 1:30 a.m., reads:

> List of things to do while in the Big Apple
> 1. Letterman
> 2. Click and Elite
> 3. MOMA, Met, Whitney
> 4. *Les Miserables*
> 5. Audition for *Cats*
> 6. Check out *Sassy, Rolling Stone, Details,* and *Premiere*
> 7. Buy shoes on 8th Avenue

I have yet to "do" *Les Miz* or Letterman, but I did subject myself to the humiliation of drop-in day at Elite and other modeling agencies. I even suited up for a *Cats* cattle call. I visited museums, too, and learned that the shoe stores are on Eighth *Street,* not Eighth Avenue. That list, full of misunderstood directions and out-of-hand rejection, might have been all I came to know of New York had I not had the grounding experience of entering the world of *Ms.,* which demanded new skills from me (faxing, clearing paper jams) and provided a social milieu not so different from a 1970s consciousness-raising group.

Yes, I was an unpaid intern at the one big feminist magazine. *Ms.,* where the letters-to-the-editor section ran for pages and tended to drip with gratitude. *Ms.* of the "no ads, please, we're feminist." *Ms.* of the all-female staff and no dress code. *Ms.* of the (who knew?) male owner with vexing financial problems who also owned *Sassy*, the avant-garde teen magazine with great style and cool young editors such as Kim France and Christina Kelly. Gloria Steinem's *Ms.*— *that* one. To a just-graduated, intense college feminist who spent her undergrad years planning antipornography forums, when not drinking the free beer at frat parties, *Ms.* was Mecca. We even did a pornography issue a few months into my tenure that had all the range of opinion I had mustered at my college porn forum—which is to say, from Andrea Dworkin to Andrea Dworkin. Being in the *Ms.* offices, even as an unpaid lackey, meant entering the serious, real work world. I would never have to say *"Hospitaliano!"* or any other Olive Garden/Chili's/Red Lobster greeting again.

Or, not exactly. Since I was an unpaid intern, to pay the bills, I got a job waitressing at a macho West Village writers' haunt called the Lion's Head, on Christopher Street and Seventh Avenue. It was garden level and murky—even at noon—with a huge oak bar and the kind of air that is best described as visible. In 1993, the Lion's Head was a New York institution, albeit a crumbling one, where old newspaper guys such as Jimmy Breslin and Pete Hamill drank, or maybe they were sober then but they still hung out in the bar, holding court beneath their framed book jackets adorning the walls. The bartenders were dyspeptic old guys with beards who wrote poetry, took themselves very seriously, and treated me like shit: "Whatayastupid? 'Up' and 'neat' are the same thing!!" Like shit, that is, until the next new girl was hired. Then, according to some tribal New York restaurant code, they loved me: "Sweetheart, make sure you get home safe—alright, Fargo? Where's that dim-bulb new girl?"

Grizzled white men poured drinks and dispensed dubious wisdom. Young white women in tight clothes delivered the food and the smiles and said "sorry" all the time. Short brown men cooked it all and cleaned it all up, and still managed to rise above the racial oppression of the United States to make kissing sounds at us waitresses whenever we were in the kitchen. The Lion's Head was nothing like *Ms.*, where an editor apologized to an intern for five minutes before sheepishly asking her to make a photocopy.

I lived downtown from *Ms.* and east of the Lion's Head, in the twenties, just shy of tony Gramercy Park and a few blocks from a playhouse where *Oleanna*, David Mamet's drama of PC feminism run amok, was playing. My friend Karen had seen the play and reported that after the climactic scene in which the professor punches the witch-hunting female student who ruined his life, the audience became positively barbaric: "Kill the bitch!" one woman yelled. Grumpy bartenders and David Mamet, modeling agencies and walking down the street to a catcall serenade of *"Mami"* and "Give me a smile, sweetheart"—it all struck me as exciting and sexist. So satisfying to be furious about. So teeming with sexual politics. "Figures of male authority aroused in me a confusing medley of corked fury and hunger to please," as Jon Krakauer writes in *Into the Wild*. I was furious. I was hungry.

Four months into New York City, life changed. I was hired full-time by *Ms.* magazine to be the internship coordinator for a sum of four hundred dollars a week; I kept my restaurant job one night a week. By day, I faxed contracts and research to the likes of radical-feminist law professor Catharine MacKinnon, at work on a piece about rape camps in Bosnia. By night, I brought Kaliber nonalcoholic beers and steak *au poivre* to people like Lou Reed and fended off guys who'd show up to walk me home at the end of my shift at 3:00 a.m. My days and nights were like night and day—feminist enclave versus masculine den—so different, but each with its own extreme charms and allure.

New York City was big enough to hold both worlds and

many more. I marveled at the gargoyles on the architecture, at how every residential building looked like a giant advent calendar and I could peek into each window to observe a new diorama. I had found my way to Eighth Street (between Fifth and Sixth Avenues) and bought a pair of Dr. Martens boots to wear waitressing and walking to and from the magazine. My love life was still a one-way street. I made out on a pool table with a long-haired guy from college named Tom. I slept with a WASP named Jim, who took me to my first black-tie affair. I pined after my doe-eyed ex-boyfriend, Brian, even though he was kind of a loser, pot-smoking pizza delivery boy. I passive-aggressively fended off Greg, the reporter who rammed his tongue down my throat every time he saw me. I sort of returned the affections of gorgeous, smart lawyer Charlie from college. I got attention from Hank and guys from the Lion's Head who seemed gay but kept asking me out. There were plenty of men in my life, but no one I really connected with, no one that great.

So that was 1993.

Here's what I saw when I looked the other way:

Alongside images of Tom, Jim, Brian, and the gang, imagine that *Ms.* intern I mention on the first page of this book. She had black curls and poreless skin and the extravagant name of Anastasia Higginbotham. She worked at the Paramount Hotel as office manager of housekeeping, even though she was just twenty-one, fresh out of Vanderbilt University, and had no previous experience. If you know anything about the Paramount in the early 1990s, you know that it was and still is a chic yet cramped Ian Schrager hotel with interiors designed by Philippe Starke and frequented by rock stars and Johnny Depp types when they were in the city. One of Anastasia's jobs was to rent porn for the guests, which we found totally repellant. ("Correction," Anastasia used to say. "*Thirty percent* of my job is to rent porn.") She, too, wore chunky black boots every day. They may have been in style in general or in style only at *Ms.*; either way, we regarded them as vital tools in our fight against the patriarchy. They were tough-looking, good for your feet, and easy to get around in. Critiquing high heels as something the patriarchy had invented to keep women helpless was a big part of my feminism then.

I met Anastasia one Monday in the *Ms.* intern vestibule, surrounded by posters touting BETTY concerts and pro-choice rallies. *Ms.* may have been chic philosophically, but its offices were dingy. Stacks of manuscripts under every chipped brown Formica desk, cast-off chairs, and no natural light—a less-than-cushy setting I have come to think of as typically feminist. (I.e., if it's comfortable, it's not feminist—unless of course we're talking about shoes.) Anastasia had just begun her internship (while I was away on a family trip), and I had been intending to introduce myself before tackling the slush pile, which was usually two feet high and filled with incest narratives.

Anastasia was answering a phone call when I walked in. As she turned around, I felt a *zzzt!*—a pang of something electric and alive. She had silvery blue eyes and a slightly shaggy pixie cut with errant tendrils curling around her ears. Her teeth were noticeably adorable, and she smiled with her mouth open a little bit, as if she were about to bite into a blueberry. I remember that I didn't go through my usual female checklist ("Her hair is cuter, but mine is blonder," etc.). I just loved looking at her. It turned out she was very funny and drew comic strips with alternative Barbie scenarios (nine frames of female masochism with the tagline "And you thought her *tits* were scary!"). She was also extremely earnest—a word I never truly understood until I worked at *Ms.* Vanderbilt and her Catholic upbringing had driven Anastasia to cut off her long hair and invest in the boots. At school, she'd taken an off-campus witchcraft class disguised as a Women and Religion course, though its goddess-y name—"Cakes for the Queen of Heaven"—gave away its true nature.

I hadn't really had any conscious attraction to women up until that point in my life. I didn't know then what I know now: that sexual and romantic same-sex relationships are very common among straight-identified women of my generation and younger, and that feminism (in the form of our raised expectations and our freedoms) probably has a lot to do with that. I didn't yet know that my best friend in college was having an affair with her female roommate for three out of our four years. Or that my old voice teacher from Fargo was now living with a woman. Another pal hadn't yet called off her engagement to a guy and moved in with a single mother/cabaret star. I couldn't have foreseen that in 2000 my college roommate's mother would get divorced and marry a woman in Hawaii. I didn't have the vision to look back at all of my own moments and put two and two together. All those massages with the neighbor girl in high school; how bereft I felt when my friend from dance class (the ditzy blonde who slept over every night in 1985) had to go live with her dad for the summer.

In my memory, my two "serious" boyfriends had dominated ninth through twelfth grade. First there was John, with whom I behaved like some crazy Joan Collins viper instead of admitting I didn't know how to French kiss, much less how to have a good "relationship." Then there was Tim, who was shorter than I and had a beautiful tenor voice. There was also sexy-but-cheating Brady, whom I couldn't stay away from in college and is now a very trustworthy father of three in Madison, Wisconsin. In New York, there was plenty of attention from and fun with guys. No one I was writing home about, but people to kiss and get flirty with.

But perhaps I was more invested in what women were all

about than I remember. That same journal entry I quoted earlier, about the *Cats* audition, also includes this glimpse into my twenty-two-year-old 1993 psyche: "*Ms.* is fucking cool. The office is 75 percent lesbian. I am in the minority as a straight Midwestern girl."

I think it's safe to say I was a little titillated by the Sapphic traffic at my new job. *Ms.* was at no time 75 percent lesbian—maybe 30 percent, tops. I don't think I was in the minority being from the Midwest, actually, and, as it turned out, I was hardly the straight girl I envisioned myself to be. *Ms.* was my first contact with lesbians—and these had cool girlfriends and good jobs (i.e., lives I related to and pined after). Even the straight women on the staff didn't spend a lot of time gossiping about men. It was the first time I *truly* saw women without men as being successes, not failures. I had mouthed this rhetoric before, but had always secretly felt a little vulnerable without some guy around to demonstrate that I was lovable. Women without men loomed large in my new world. Maybe that's why I thought so many of them were lesbians.

The whole *Ms.* staff loved Anastasia because she was competent, sexy, and delightful, and she brought in homemade snacks during tough closings. I wanted to cut to the front of the line of people getting her attention. And I did. By the time her three-month internship was over, she and I had spent so much time together that we were best friends—possessively so. The type who showers people with love and attention, she drew an extended series of cartoons about us called "Lengthy and Squiggly," based on Lenny and Squiggy from *Laverne and Shirley*, poking fun at our height difference. She wrote me hundreds of letters and faxes and cards with goddess imagery on them. She also quoted *The Simpsons* the way some people quote the Bible, in order to prove any point, and I loved that she thought TV could be funny and philosophical, just as I did ("Alcohol

is both the cause, and the solution, to all life's problems."
—Homer Simpson). She always seemed to be playing with
my long hair or refilling my water bottle or getting cookies
for us to share after 4:00 p.m., when they were three for a
dollar at the overpriced Italian restaurant across the street.
We researched the porn issue together and cased the sex
shops that used to line Times Square. We danced at a kiss-in
for the Lesbian Avengers in Grand Central. We walked
home arm in arm from work, laughing and singing Barbra
Streisand's hit "No More Tears (Enough Is Enough)" at the
top of our lungs. ("It's raining, it's pouring, my love life is
boring me to tears, after all these years.")

That June happened to be the twenty-fifth anniversary of
the Stonewall rebellion, the Lollapalooza of gay pride. A quar-
ter century earlier, the West Village had erupted in riots when
police tried to launch a night of routine humiliation for the
drag queens, butch lesbians, and blue-collar gay men who frequented the Stonewall Inn. In 1994, though, women like me
and my straight sister Andrea and anyone we were friends
with thought nothing of strolling down Fifth Avenue for the
dyke march, shoulder to shoulder with shirtless women sport-
ing stickers slapped over their nipples reading WE RECRUIT.

At work, we jokingly referred to Ms.'s hothouse environment as the Bisexual Internship Program, and many a
straight intern left with a notch in her lipstick lesbian case.
In this new world—a world full of women I was trying to
impress and one in which homophobia was not on the
menu—I found myself thinking I might be bisexual (why
not?) even before Anastasia and I got together. After all, she
had fallen in love with her best friend in college while
working on a feminist newspaper called Muliebrity (its
clunky name still makes me laugh), a 1592 word meaning
both femininity and "mulish." The fact that this girlie-girl
(boots and bravado aside) had slept with a woman made me
think I probably could, too.

One night Anastasia and I found ourselves in a straight bar called Tom and Jerry's, on Houston and Elizabeth Street, drunk and with me practically sitting on her lap. Our friend Julie Felner, one of the compelling *Ms.* lesbians, had just left us. It was 2:00 a.m. "Me and Bobby McGee" was on the jukebox and I was singing my best Janis Joplin into her ear—"freedom's just another word for nothing left to lose"—when I kissed her.

The entire noisy, grotesque, jabbering bar receded and all I could hear was her skin. Or maybe I was smelling it. I don't know. It was very disorienting. I do recall that my hand went directly to her breasts, proving to me that women's breasts are so hyper-eroticized that even people who have their own are fascinated by them. I could feel her downy mustache, which she bleaches, feathery against my upper lip.

I felt a tap on my shoulder, and a woman said, "I don't think this is the safest situation for you." She gestured at the semicircle of guys around us making no effort to conceal that this was a show for them. The two of us stumbled out of there and made our way to our separate homes, laughing really hard at the spectacle we had made. I felt sort of goofy and in love. On Monday at *Ms.*, though, I felt awkward and nervous to see her. She swept into the office holding a stack of photocopies, pointed her finger at me, and exclaimed, "You sang 'Me and Bobby McGee' in my ear!"

"I know!" I shrieked, laughing so hard I crumpled in a heap on the industrial office carpet. I almost wet my pants with embarrassment and hysteria, but I was also relieved that we were still okay.

The following Friday, Anastasia and I slept together for the first time.

At first it was just a terrific, exciting love affair that I didn't want to "label," except in the most Feminism 101 terms, although I quickly embraced the fact that I was indeed bisexual. My friend Erin, another *Ms.*-er, and I started a bisexual zine in which she focused on Kathleen Hanna of the group Bikini Kill while I wrote bisexual theories. I wanted Anastasia and me to be best friends who were also sleeping together, but I wanted my straight identity, too. I wanted to date men, kiss men, hit on men, have sex with men. Men didn't feel wrong; it's just that Anastasia felt right, too. Our relationship felt like brave new territory—without rules by nature of being outside the heterosexual norm. And this freedom helped fuel a blossoming ideology that was forming in my brain in which bisexuality was the practice of feminism. I could take what I learned from what I felt was my more liberated relationship with Anastasia and apply it to relations with men. *Presto!* Instant egalitarianism.

I admit, this ideology also helped me justify our relationship, because it also made me anxious at times to be with a woman. Sometimes, though, we were really together—like soul mates. I experienced things I'd never associated with relationships before. Things like baking Syrian bread together and dancing around the apartment to Madonna or borrowing each other's clothes. Like writing letters with elaborate drawings and photocopying Marge Piercy poems for each other. Things like orgasms.

Amid all this fulfillment, I also felt a sense of dissatisfaction that was unique, as if I were reading a scintillating novel with every other page missing. Being with her was different from being with a guy. We were so supportive of each other, but I didn't really know how to admire her—if she looked really gorgeous one night, it was distracting to me rather than alluring. When a feeling of competitiveness—be it sexual or in terms of our writing—came into the picture, it felt as awful as it did with my friends, but much more destructive. I also felt unmoored in bed—even with the orgasms—because I couldn't imagine what we looked like together or what I looked like to her. My sense of how hot and foxy a lover found me during sex had always been one of life's great pleasures, and now I had trouble believing that this other girl would or could objectify me. (And for this book, I define *objectify* as "to take in and enjoy visually"—as in a piece of art or, I suppose, a piece of ass.)

For the next two years, I dated Anastasia on and off. I vividly recall sitting on the floor at a *Ms.* editorial meeting and being able to sense when she had entered the room without turning my head to look. Our connection was very alive to me. At the office our relationship was without social or employment consequences, by virtue of *Ms.*'s pro-lesbian/pro-feminist stance. On the streets, however, sometimes it was safer for us to walk around holding hands like two giggly friends who both happened to be girls. This confused matters, though. Men still asked one or the other of us out because they believed our camouflage. *I* even often believed the camouflage. I had to explain to people all the time who Anastasia was to me, and when I didn't, she felt misunderstood or invisible. I also remember frequently thinking that I wanted us to break up—just not now. When we did break up, twice, I was always eager for us to get back together. I was horrifyingly jealous when she dated other people (always men) and suffused with bitterness when I didn't get the doting attention I'd come to expect from her. Misogyny suddenly made more sense to me, because I occasionally wanted to make her feel small when I felt rejected. Sometimes I had nothing but contempt for her and her annoying, passive-aggressive, doormat ways. I loved her generous Italian mamma side but it could also be stifling.

We broke up in 1996, suddenly, when she left me for a more confirmed lover of women named Marge—which, coincidentally, is an old slang term for lesbian.[2] Marge was older, gayer, she played softball, and she left *her* girlfriend for Anastasia—so they had two wrecked homes upon which to build theirs. I was sure that they were having much better sex than I was capable of and I felt like a totally disappointing, Little League lesbian.

Breaking up is always full of trauma and self-doubt, but this was easily the saddest and most vulnerable that I had ever felt. I still can hardly look at the letters I wrote in the aftermath of our final split: they were the linguistic equivalent of ripping one's skin off and attempting to do the same to an unwilling partner, topped off by highly desperate last-ditch efforts at seduction. Because the acceptance I got from Anastasia had seemed so complete—I could be my whole goofy self around her, something I had had a hard time doing with men—her rejection was much more dangerous to my self-esteem. Complicating matters, I had been flirting with someone else the whole time I was with Anastasia. That fact, and because I had never been able to imagine setting up house with her, made me feel sure that I had sown the seeds of our failure. *Of course she left me for Marge*, I thought: *I'm homophobic! I should have reveled in her body more! I hated her when she got more attention than I did! Maybe I was jealous of her writing?* Then I got into therapy and became angry at her for being a cheater.

Looking back on my meeting Anastasia and my transformation into an AC/DC feminist, I realize that though I was attracted to her immediately, it probably wouldn't have moved into *love* and a relationship without the same-sex feminist atmosphere of *Ms.* Women were valuable at *Ms.*, and that, along with the fact that Anastasia had already tread bisexual terrain, provided an invitation I didn't want to refuse. As scared as I felt by the identity shift, I also felt that there was little to lose. Kissing women was encouraged here: in New York and at *Ms.* It was also allowed in this place in time. In fact, days before we smooched, a pop song by Jill Sobule hit the airwaves called "I Kissed a Girl." For years, women's magazines from *Bust* to *Bitch* to *Allure* to *Jane* have chronicled how ostensibly straight women check out other women and how we quite possibly dress for one another more than for men. More recently, the cloying term *girl crush* has popped up in articles from *The New York Observer* to the shelter magazine *Domino*. Like *metrosexual* before it, *girl crush* indicated dipping into some of the fun of being gay without having to be, you know, gay. This sort of checking out and admiring is not necessarily bisexual, but it points to the fact that we women are drawn to one another in search of various intimacies. It's the rare man (even among supposed metrosexuals) who can so satisfyingly acknowledge the details of your outfit the way a woman can.

Steven was one of that distinctive breed. (Note: my male lovers didn't give me permission to use their last names.) One of the first things he ever said to me was, "Have you seen what Tom Ford is doing for Gucci? I *live* for it." One night he took in my outfit of worn-out Levi's and a light blue men's oxford and said, "That's how I'd dress you if I dressed you"—and I felt so sexy and pleasurably appreciated by him, I remember thinking, *Let's get married.* I know it sounds as if he were gay himself, but he was Scottish and part of the seventies generation of UK kids whose lives were saved by punk rock. He had been in an influential Scottish band as a teen. He knew style; he understood its importance, but not in a stupid label-conscious way. We met when I was twenty-four, about a year after I met Anastasia. He was a decade older than I and was editing a book about store-bought counterculture, which he referred to as "over-the-counter culture." I loved the way he cringed when he talked about piercings and Bobby Brady T-shirts and Japanese Manga comics—as if he were already out of the demographic and too dignified to pretend any different. I also liked his vocabulary (stunning), his body (waifish), his accent (Glaswegian), and his sense of humor (self-deprecating). E-mail was more common by the time I began doing some writing for his book (1995) and he'd occasionally sign his cyber missives "perfumed regards." Encounters with Steven left me blushing for three days.

About six months before Anastasia left me for the real lesbian, I initiated a too-intense friendship with him, and once Anastasia and I had actually split, I threw myself into dating him. *Must make dastardly flirtation worth hideous breakup*, was my mantra—but in truth, I was really taken with him. Steven was my first big male love since I started thinking of myself as not quite straight. He had huge pond-colored eyes and was sharp as a knife, and when he really relaxed and smiled, he looked as innocent and full of hope as he must have at age ten. My idea of fun was rolling around with him on his Kelly green couch all afternoon.

My attraction to him was heightened by what I had missed while dating Anastasia—namely, sex with a man's body. I also wanted heterosexual dating and privileges, I didn't want to be so polite and processed, I didn't want to worry about being gay-bashed, and I wanted to be with someone who wasn't so similar to me out in the world. Anastasia and I had bonded deeply over telling off our street harassers. Steven wasn't getting cat-calls. Or if he was, we weren't bonding over it, which I found refreshing. I wanted someone from whose mouth the word *panties* sounded like we were going to have sex, not like we were at a bachelorette party. (I have since met women in whose mouths the word translates as dirty, so that Rubicon is crossable from either side.) We were different on the streets and in the sheets, but there was one realm in which I craved similarity. Steven was an up-and-coming magazine writer, and I wanted to be one, too. He had power (to my mind) in the glamorous world of regular magazines, as opposed to ad-free, bimonthly feminist magazines. By this time, my vision of "*Ms.* as utopia" had been eaten by its alter ego, "*Ms.* as ghetto." I wanted what he had almost as much as I wanted him.

Sadly, with Steven, good times were few and far between. I began to think of our relationship as akin to living in Portland—it usually rains, but when it's sunny, God, you appreciate it. Most of the time he was depressed and unable to show up for anything, from a movie date to see *Austin Powers* to Indian food with my gang. He didn't like many of my friends. He didn't relate to my political interests. In 1996, when I asked him to a gay marriage rally organized by my friend Susan Buttenweiser, he said, "I'm not the rally type"— which made me worry that he couldn't appreciate or participate in "my" world and that our common world (the world of the *B*s: Barneys, Burt Bacharach, Sandra Bernhard) was just too small. But the good times felt *really* good. Like our jag of having sex all the time, during which he described his constant state of arousal as feeling like he had "hot butter in his veins." Like the night at a dinner party where he was complaining about how boring pop music was and I said there was one new album that had struck a chord in me, and he responded, "*Pinkerton* by Weezer?"—and he was *right*. Or the Thanksgiving we had in my tiny apartment, when he seemed so happy and I was so proud of making a turkey and a pumpkin pie and he even listened to Dar Williams and got maudlin with me and my sister. ("I never should have rented this apartment / in the mortal city . . ." we all sang, drunkenly.) When it worked, it worked. When it didn't? Well, I came to think of him as the cold, distant father I never had.

If I had to greatly simplify the problem, I would say I had "gay expectations": I wanted him to be my partner but I had very little confidence in my ability to have an "equal" relationship with a man. I wanted to have the intimacy I had felt with Anastasia from a man who I worried was an old-school, can't-teach-an-old-dog-new-tricks type of guy. Another issue was about bisexuality. He was very comfortable (as in he never mentioned it, really) that my ex was a girl, yet he appeared to have no stake in gay rights.

One night we went on a double date with my friend Marcelle and a friend of Steven's whose name I don't recall; we were hooking them up. It was late winter 1996, around the time President Clinton had signed the Defense of Marriage Act, which stated preemptively that marriage is between a man and a woman, in case anyone hadn't noticed that already. Steven's friend remarked that he didn't have anything against gays, but he definitely didn't think they should be allowed to get married. My throat tightened. I debated with him for a while in a cajoling tone, waiting for Marcelle or Steven to back me up. Finally, feeling alone, I decided to go for the extreme: "Look, *I'm* gay. This is not an abstraction to me. You are saying that if I fall in love with a woman and want to get married, I can't." Steven looked at me as if I had said, "Look, I'm from Mars. My robot Zorc and I would like to get hitched."

At dinner's end, I headed out to hail a cab. The wind whipped up suddenly, in that dramatic, prairie way so common in New York, where you are almost lifted off the sidewalk from the gale force. Steven was chilly and flat in his own dramatic, prairie way and refused to come home with me. I called him later, mad that I had been left to defend gay marriage to his stupid friend but also feeling as if I had screwed something up permanently. He said, "All I could think when you said you were 'gay' was, then *who am I to you?*"

Who *was* he to me? I wanted Steven for my boyfriend, although I had developed an aversion to that term, with its conjuring images of "typical" couples who bicker in public and women who make compromises to protect menfolk's fragile egos. We broke up for a while during the summer, and I missed him badly. I tried to date other people to wrench myself from this grumpy, withholding, and utterly compelling man, but none compared. I wanted Steven but I hated how our relationship made me feel: like an idiot, a needy, theatrically political idiot.

During that particularly ragged time with Steven, I met Amy Ray, the low-voiced brunette half of the Indigo Girls, while on assignment for *Ms.* magazine. (Yes, *Ms.* is my female dating service.) Despite her feminist politics and her femaleness, Amy's presence was unlike Anastasia's; in fact, she was more like Steven to me. She was older and had at her disposal what I think of as male privilege (lots of money and respect, plus she could play guitar). She and her singing partner, Emily Saliers, had a unique stage presence. They never sat on folk-singer stools, but instead stood looking out directly at the crowd. They played incredibly loud, and when you witness their power and strength you realize suddenly just how passive the image of the chick with the acoustic guitar sitting on the damn stool is. Elizabeth Wurtzel, the author of *Prozac Nation* and *Bitch*, has described Amy as "awash with lust" and a woman who is not "obedient to the male gaze." If *that* wasn't enough, while Amy had curves and was clearly all woman, her growly voice and jeans-and-boots uniform was more butch than the attire of my fey boyfriend, Steven. Amy reeked of liberation and toughness; yet she could also be vulnerable and languid, like a kitten—a gorgeous feral kitten. She's that bad boy you want, but in a girl who believes in recycling. Freud described the kinds of feelings I had for Amy as loving the same person twice, as a woman and as a man.[3]

I was still in love with Steven, but the second I saw Amy in the lobby of the Missoula, Montana, Doubletree Inn, I knew that I wanted her. Backstage after the Indigo Girls concert that night, I told Amy that one of the security guards had asked me if I was her girlfriend. She could tell it was a pick-up line and moved closer. Standing eye to eye with me, she said in a husky Southern voice, "I don't have a girlfriend." I made a mental note of that.

Despite the fact that Steven was in the picture, my mind kept wandering back to Amy. She was very forward about her feelings and her past—she talked about having been in love with a bisexual rocker I admired; she talked about having fallen for a straight activist I knew. Clearly, she didn't mind quasi-lesbians. I talked up my relationship with Anastasia, going so far as to send her a comic Anastasia drew of the two of us in our underwear. (A figment of Anastasia's imagination, but very suggestive nonetheless.) We began talking on the phone at all hours. I told her she could call as late as she wanted. I somehow failed to mention Steven.

Simultaneously, I was suddenly having the kind of relationship with Steven I had always wanted—one in which I felt happy and confident and free and respected. When I had a cold, he brought me white grape juice and T. Rex records; I bought him dishes for his bachelor pad so that he no longer lived like a guest in his own home. He suddenly showed interest in all of my friends and my family. When he remarked that he feared he was pussy-whipped, my sister said, no, he was "pussy-equipped"—meaning ready for a relationship—and it seemed as if he was reveling in the fact that he felt generous and virile and devoted to me. In spite of this love, sex, and equality with Steven, I didn't want to let go of Amy. More than that, I sensed that the good stuff I was having with Steven had something to do with what she had brought out in me. Or, more to the point, my confidence and self-knowledge about what I wanted had something to do with having a woman in my romantic sphere.

It wasn't long before I broke up with Steven and fell in love with Amy.

If I had to characterize what was missing in my relationship with Steven, I'd say it was a lack of intimacy. I had no sense that it was within my power to alter the relationship from its current script, and the disconnect I felt between the equal, confident relationship I wanted and the way I had to dance around him was torture. With Anastasia, the relating was very intimate, but too similar, too familiar. There was almost a lack of respect on my part, a bit of misogyny. Being with Anastasia was so delectable, but also, like *Ms.*, a ghetto—too confining, underresourced, and undervalued—a margin that is expected to hold too much.

It was about that time that I began pondering the problem—and the solution—of bisexuality. The reason that I didn't feel as intimate with men has something to do with how women and men are treated or valued differently in society. In his exceedingly satisfying book *The Corrections*, Jonathan Franzen describes the cost-benefit analysis I routinely do about men versus women. This thought is from Denise, the youngest of the three Lambert children, who happens to be looking both ways in her life via a torrid affair with a woman and a satisfying flirtation with the woman's husband.

> Whenever she was with Brian she would pine for Robin's body and sincerity and good works and be repelled by Brian's smug coolness, and whenever she was with Robin she would pine for Brian's good taste and like-mindedness and wish that Robin would notice how sensational she looked in black cashmere.

The Corrections came out in 2001 and immediately blew me away with its insights about Denise—a woman about my age who was exploring her sexuality and her ambitions. Both men and women were crucial to her finding her way professionally—Brian had money and entitlement; Robin inspired her. Both were crucial to her sexual awakening—Brian made her feel admired and powerful; on the other hand, she had never wanted anyone with such pure lust as she felt for Robin.

Since 1993, when I first came to New York, so much has

changed to dispel some of the most rigid ideas about gay people—in my own homophobic head, of course, but also in the culture at large. Most of the change can be explained by one word: *visibility*. The AIDS crisis provided a national stage for discussions about gay rights, and a full range of gay activists came to the fore—the Log Cabin yuppies as well as the dykes on bikes. Ellen DeGeneres told the world she was gay (although some of us already knew that) when her show was at the height of its popularity, and brought a familiar and loved visage to the scary debate. Melissa Etheridge and her former partner Julie Cypher were featured in the "Couples" section of *People* magazine after they had their kids, and were treated, at least in those pages, just like any celebrity couple. Cypher and Etheridge were also on the cover of *Rolling Stone*, with an accompanying article revealing that David Crosby had provided the contents of their inseminating turkey baster. Among other things, the *Rolling Stone* story was a consciousness-raising session on the how-tos of lesbian procreation. In the nineties, there was hardly a television show without a major gay character or plot line, from *All My Children* to *Will and Grace*, or a popular novel's plot without a sexuality twist. In 2002, I noted *The Corrections, The Hours,* and *Look at Me* among the year's best-sellers. In 2005 teen television was awash in the phenomenon: *One Tree Hill* and *The OC* both had a bisexual female main character. Gay marriage is the most consciously acknowledged civil rights struggle of this generation, sparking heated debates on the Hill and in our homes. We are in a cultural moment of optimum momentum—even my grandma in Fargo knows about gay people; even my conservative Fargo high school now has a gay-straight alliance.

In the sixties and seventies, feminism enabled women to "come into" lesbianism and bisexuality by experimenting with or adopting new identities. After all, feminism was a powerful new movement dedicated to valuing women. It also provided venues for women to meet one another, at events ranging from political meetings to protests to dances. The gay rights movement benefited greatly from feminism, with the radical gay rights/anti-AIDS group ACT UP and the Gay Men's Health Crisis borrowing their methods directly from breast cancer activists. Nowadays, I would argue that it's the gay-lesbian-bisexual-transgendered movement, rather than the feminist movement, that is ascendant. For the first time ever, more than half of Fortune 500 companies currently offer same-sex partner benefits, a number that leapt from only twenty-one companies in the mid-1990s. In that same period colleges and universities offering same-sex partner benefits have nearly quadrupled, from 77 to 290.[4] Today the gay rights movement provides new energy and light for the goals of the feminist movement: it makes it clear that domestic tasks do not have to be divided according to gender, and that children aren't psychologically scarred when their last names are hyphenated. (Or at least less scarred than I was, for instance, by my mother singing folk songs at my school in second grade.) It is the GLBT movement that is changing the world *right now*—as opposed to feminism, which is embedded in our culture and laws, and in many ways is much less visible.

And yet, what is still usually invisible, within all of the rampant visibility that gay rights has achieved, is the insurgent role of bisexual people. Because we are a part of the mainstream, the alternative margin, and the gaystream (the mainstreaming of queer life), we have empathy for and insight into the straight and queer worlds. Bisexual people are the primary conduits for the cultural conversation that America is having about gay rights. Like it or not, Ellen's coming out would have been a lot less decisive without an entitled former straight girl named Anne, who insisted right off the bat that Ellen was her wife.

CHAPTER 2

WHAT IS BISEXUALITY?

That same part of her was thinking also: My God, the ways she eats. *And:* I am not a lesbian.

—Denise Lambert, from Jonathan Franzen's *The Corrections*

I have a recurring dream where I'm at a family wedding and I can hear my mother's voice ringing out over the throng, "Jenny's a bisexual. Jenny's a bisexual," while I smile wanly. Of course, I want my loved ones to know who I am. The act of admitting who you are not only invites others to do that too, but it also frees you from living a double life—or worse, a vague life. Therefore, no sooner had my lips met another woman's than I wanted my family to be up on my evolution. I hadn't been in New York City for much more than a year when I wrote my mother, in a letter she received the day before Mother's Day, to say that I was *bisexual*. Mother remembers it this way:

> I have always said that I don't care about a gift, I just want a Mother's Day card and I want it to be there on time. But that year you all missed the date and instead I got this letter and no cards. I was a little surprised by your letter, but I wasn't completely bowled over because at Christmastime you girls had been asking me whether *I* had ever wanted to kiss a girl. And when I said, "No," you

insisted, "Oh, you must have wanted to at some sleepover or at some point." But I really hadn't.

Contemplating this maternal recollection some years later, I
think I had been terrified that my experience might not be
common—and I would be marginalized and alone. I recall
that I meant the confessional letter to be casual: *This is not a
bombshell.* I was committed to setting the tone, and the tone
was instructive and confident. I didn't want this to be *that*
coming-out story where the girl tells her parents and they
are disappointed and kick her out of the house, nor did I
want it to be the one where the parents show tearful acceptance and go run the local chapter of PFLAG. I wanted
everything to be the same as it was before, just with my girlfriend in the picture. Besides, 90 percent of me believed that
my making out with a woman was no big deal and that I
should *not* encourage any parental weirdness by asking how
they felt, as if I were waiting for approval. But, of course, in
a way I *was* waiting for acceptance. Ten percent of me was
afraid of my parents' disapproval, as indicated by my writing
my mother a letter as if it were 1875 and the telephone
hadn't been invented yet.

My parents are an odd combination of conventional and
liberal—the Cleavers meet Paul and Linda McCartney. My
mother is a former homecoming queen named Cindy who
still keeps in touch with her high school gang and who
seemed radical when I was a kid in Fargo because she made
Greek salad for dinner and subscribed to *Ms.* magazine. Dad
is a Clint Eastwood–looking jock who was the only member
of his ten-person family to go to college. He has a "favorite"
Prince song, "Sometimes It Snows in April," which I think
conveys his sensitivity nicely. My parents met in seventh
grade. My father fell for my mother the minute he saw her
flouncing down the hall of South Junior High in Grand
Forks, North Dakota, all gigantic, buck-toothed smile and

fearless popularity. They married at twenty-one and are still in love.

Mom's response to my revelation when we finally spoke on Mother's Day was interesting. "Do you have a problem with your dad?" she asked. It was an old-fashioned notion, which my mother told me later had to do with having never thought about bisexuality before in her life. Then, she said, "Are you rejecting the kind of life I chose?" And, then, as the conversation moved from her to me: "The only bisexual I can think of is . . . Elton John," she said, in a mulling-it-over tone. "And he seems so *unstable*."

This was before Anne Heche, and while she's not entirely easy to relate to either, it's harder to make yourself understood when Elton John is the most visible example of who you think you are. The phone call transpired during Elton John's *Tantrums & Tiaras* phase, when it was reported that the once-married John spent an average of two thousand dollars a day on flowers and needed sixteen trunks to carry his wardrobe when he traveled, even for only a weekend in Bermuda. I think he may have also been in rehab.

Mom's other fears I could dispense with confidently. I didn't have a problem with my dad and I didn't disrespect my mother. In a way, the stability of their marriage was part of what made me feel I could eschew a more conventional path. I didn't need to make up for what they hadn't given me. Despite my quick—even pat—answers to Mom's instinctive concerns, I now realize that her real questions were What is bisexuality? What does it mean?

My mother isn't the only person wondering. Researchers strapping penile sensors on men watching porn, attempting to measure bisexual desire, want to know. The cultural critic Elizabeth Wurtzel wants to know. So does that *Details* editor. And I'm certainly wondering. In fact, "What is bisexuality?" is one of those enormous questions that has loomed large over the cultural landscape without ever getting a satisfying answer, and falls somewhere between "Which came first, the chicken or the egg?" and "Is God dead?" Bisexuality, especially among women, is a phenomenon people tend to just know about—we can all refer to it sophisticatedly, with a smirk, when we hear that the neighbor girl went to Mount Holyoke, or with misty-eyed platitudes such as "Deep down, aren't we all bisexual?" We know, and yet we don't know.

Webster's dictionary is not so helpful; the first two definitions are essentially "hermaphrodite" and the third is "sexually attracted by both sexes." I Googled *bisexual* and learned from the BiNet Web site that "a bisexual is someone who has the ability to be sexually attracted to men and women." According to Robyn Ochs, the editor of *Getting Bi: Voices of Bisexuals Around the World* and an activist for more than twenty-five years, "a bisexual person has the potential to be sexually and/or romantically attracted to more than one sex, but not necessarily at the same time or to the same extent." A more social definition of bisexuality is provided by bisexual icon Lani Ka'ahumanu, in *The Reader's Companion to U.S. Women's History*: "Bisexuals are a part of as well as apart from heterosexual society and the lesbian and gay community."

Rather than defined, bisexuals have been "treated," as in therapized, since the Victorian Era. No one examined bisexuality—or at least bisexuals—more than Sigmund Freud. Feminists have critiqued Freud's sexism, and feminist relational psychologists have shown that despite Freud's assertions, physical drives aren't simply or exclusively what motivate human beings. Still, when it comes to bisexuality, Freud was there early, and his style—talk therapy—enabled him to learn that sexuality was much more complex than polite company would allow, and that both sexual abuse and sexual "deviance" were very common.

Born May 6, 1856, in Freiberg, Germany, Freud was not

just the father of psychoanalysis but also the doting mother of bisexuality. If it's true (as Nietzsche believed) that phi-losophers tend to write their memoirs in their theories, Freud, the man, was not unfamiliar with the concept of looking both ways himself. His friend Wilhelm Fliess was the object of Freud's most breathless and profound corre-spondence—and the provocateur of his greatest insights. Freud referred to Fliess as his only Other, his Daemon, and breathlessly declared Fliess's praise "nectar and ambrosia" to him.[5]

Freud accepted the fact that many men preferred to spend their time with other men. In one essay, he approv-ingly observed homosociality, describing how men left the company of one another in school to marry, but rushed to join the gentleman's club the moment they tired of domes-tic life. Freud was an intellectual, a doctor, and he believed he was on the scent of paradigm-shifting research. Women in the late 1800s were rarely as educated as he, nor did they contribute "serious" work to society—it was natural that he'd turn to men for his intellectual fix. Freud wrote that love and work were the cornerstones of humanness, which strikes me as true, except that I see these two fundamentals as often intertwined—a braided rope of humanness rather than two distant stones.

Freud's wife, Martha, was certainly not his confidante, and was no longer his partner in that one act wives were ex-pected to engage in. When Freud first became close with Fliess, he confessed that he and Martha were abstaining from sex in order to give her a break from constant child-bearing. Martha had had six kids in nine years and ran a bustling household. The demands of domesticity were so great that she "virtually made Fliess necessary," according to Freud's definitive biographer, Peter Gay, in a rather cold assessment. She was the dry, dedicated partner who ran

Freud's daily life so that his real love—work, and anyone who went into unraveling the mysteries of the mind with him—could be nurtured.

So, who was this muse who enabled Freud's bisexual epiphanies? Fliess was an ear, nose, and throat specialist who had several creative theories, including a belief that the nose—with its bulbous shape and inner hollows—was a sex organ. Freud suffered from nosebleeds, but was also hopelessly addicted to cigars. His nose specialist and "beloved friend" Fliess suggested that the workaholic forgo his daily cigar. A failure at quitting any vice, Freud did, for his part, hit upon a theory as to what was behind addictions such as his: displaced masturbation. What was he dreaming of as he puffed away on those phallic symbols and wrote impetuous letters to his friend? Perhaps his need *not* to know inspired his most famous maxim: "Sometimes a cigar is just a cigar."

I like to think of Freud as the mother of bisexuality because he nurtured and further developed Fliess's initial seed of bisexuality in his own fertile psyche. The version of bisexuality Fliess described to Freud was closer to what we now understand as androgyny, applied literally. For instance, Fliess said that there is a masculine and a feminine side to each of us, which might explain why some people feel an invitation to be attracted to either sex. Psychosexual health comes from males suppressing the feminine in themselves and females the masculine. Freud then brought the theory of innate bisexuality to the world, elaborating on it for the rest of his life, and denying paternity to Fliess (as the birth mother can do), "forgetting" that it was his friend who first uttered such a potent concept. Any casual student of Freud knows, though, that he believed one never forgets; one represses.

When Fliess first mentioned his theory of bisexuality to Freud in 1898, the great analyst balked at it. Within a few years, though, there was a spate of writing in European intellectual circles on the topic. In typical sexist fashion, bisexuality was used to rationalize why those few women who managed to have a creative or intellectual life were able to do so. Their masculine side was dominant, of course— blessedly, though neurotically, so. Adopting masculine traits was also seen as a way to avoid the feminine role and thus avoid having to be the helpmate rather than the main event. Otto Weininger, one such fashionable theorist, was a young, depressed misogynist and anti-Semitic scholar of Freud's acquaintance who wrote a 1904 book, *Sex and Character*, that imagined bisexuality as men and women fusing to find a perfect "whole." (His view anticipates the opening scene of *Hedwig and the Angry Inch*, the play and film about a transgendered rock chanteuse. The first number depicts original humans as man and woman together in one being, then unnaturally split apart. This idea goes all the way back to Plato's *Symposium* and the famous dinner party where all the philosophers discuss love. Aristophanes, for his part, asserts that there were originally three sexes: man, woman, and a union of the two that existed as one and was referred to as Androgynous. These unions were ultimately cleaved in two by the gods and each half is destined to search for its original other.)

According to Garber, both Weininger's and Fliess's theories gave primacy to heterosexuality even while identifying masculine and feminine principles in all of us.[6] Fliess saw in Weininger's work a near carbon copy of the theory he had shared only with Freud and that he, Fliess, had wanted to make into an historic book. When Fliess confronted his loose-lipped friend (who had indeed mentioned Fliess's insight to Weininger), Freud had already absorbed how consequential bisexuality was to the study of neurosis and the understanding of "sexuality, repression, and desire."[7] He wrote to Fliess on August 7, 1901, with clueless hubris, "And now, the main thing! As far as I can see, my next work will be called 'Human Bisexuality.' It will go to the root of the problem and say the last word it may be granted me to say—the last and the most profound."[8]

Although Freud never underwent analysis himself—something he felt everyone else needed—he did acknowledge that he had "homosexual" feelings for his former friend and suspected that Fliess's "paranoia" (stemming from the fact that Freud had purloined his best idea) was in fact Fliess's homosexual passion for Sigmund sublimated.[9]

Freud's theories about bisexuality progressed through three phases. The first was a version of Fliess's biological bisexuality: we are all born bisexual, but mature adults repress their homosexual desire and get together with opposite-sex partners. Later, he believed the root of bisexuality was in culture, not biology. Eventually, he described it as the unfixed nature of attraction and sexual identity, alluding to the fluid description of bisexuality (indeed, all sexuality) that most of today's theorists now embrace. Freud ultimately believed that sexuality changes and evolves throughout one's life, imagining that even the term *bisexuality*, as broad as it's meant to be, is inadequate to describe the drives for sex and love, as well as the deep connections we feel to certain people at certain times.

Freud's most radical legacy is the one that is the least actualized. After years of evolution on the topic, he came to the conclusion that any exclusive monosexual interest—regardless of whether it was hetero- or homosexual—was neurotic. In a sense Freud is saying what second-wave critic Kate Millett said a half century later: "Homosexuality was invented by a straight world dealing with its own bisexuality."[10] By the end of his writings, in 1937, Freud was downright blithe about bisexuality: "Every human being['s] . . . libido is distributed, either in a manifest or a latent fashion, over objects of both sexes."[11]

A decade or so later, Alfred Kinsey took Freud's idea of a

distribution of the libido and converted it into the famous Kinsey Scale. Many other experts have pondered bisexuality, from Weininger to Fritz Klein to Robyn Ochs, but Freud's and Kinsey's ideas have had the deepest impact on mainstream culture. The second major codifier of bisexuality, Kinsey was a zoologist and gall wasp specialist who taught at Indiana University in the thirties and forties. Born June 23, 1894, Kinsey was presumably forming his Oedipal complex around the time Freud was learning about bisexuality. When some female co-eds at Indiana asked if their youngish prof would teach a course on marriage and sex, he decided to give it a go.

As Kinsey researched reading materials upon which to base the course, he found that there were enormous holes in what was known about the psychological, physical, and medical understanding of sexuality. He developed a series of 350 questions and began collecting the sexual histories of his students, via face-to-face interviews rather than questionnaires. In doing so, he got their stories, instead of just their labels of sexual identity, and from this data he developed the Kinsey Scale, which rates three elements of sexuality—sexual desires, sexual practices, and sexual identity—on a continuum from 0 (exclusively straight) to 6 (exclusively gay). There are five spots on the scale that represent bisexuality. In the center sits the "Kinsey 3," representing those equally straight and gay.

Initially, Kinsey's work focused on men, for whom he found that a full 50 percent had had some bisexual experience. In 1948, he published *Sexual Behavior in the Human Male*, which was called the "least-read bestseller" because of its controversial and shockingly explicit content. Five years later, he published *Sexual Behavior in the Human Female*, finally filling the void in sexology. His study of females caused a lot more controversy than the male report, largely because it refuted assumptions about women's frigidity and virginity and demonstrated how common it was for a woman to have had an abortion. Half of the six thousand women who provided him with sexual histories said they weren't virgins when they got married, and 35 percent had had some bisexual experience.

This was the 1950s and the height of McCarthyism, so while Kinsey was breaking ground, he was also courting censure. The House Un-American Activities Committee launched an investigation, accusing Kinsey of undermining the American family and thus being a Communist, and Kinsey soon lost his Rockefeller funding. He died in 1956, but the Kinsey Institute he founded at Indiana University is still in existence, though not generating the cutting-edge sex research it once did. The huge preponderance of bisexuality that men such as Kinsey and Freud found is in steep contrast to both conventional wisdom and more recent "comprehensive" sex studies, such as *Sex in America*. *Sex in America* researchers gathered interviews from 3,432 respondents in 1992, and found that 7 percent of men and 4 percent of women reported having had some kind of same-sex encounter. (This bisexual downswing also coincided with the widespread use of Prozac and other antidepressants—also known as libido killers—so perhaps the work is more true than I think.)

Kinsey was bisexual himself, openly experimenting with many men while maintaining a lasting partnership with his wife. He also possessed the rare ability to convey a nonjudgmental attitude when conducting interviews. Did his openness and personal instincts about the fluidity of sexual attraction account for the much higher proportion of self-reported bisexuality he elicited? My guess is yes. Kinsey interviewed the way Freud conducted psychoanalysis, eliciting complicated and more honest stories, something impossible to get from a dry questionnaire or phone survey.

All of the bisexuality theorists I have come across do

what Millett, Freud, and Kinsey (not to mention Margaret Mead and Ani DiFranco) do. They assert that while bisexuality is natural and common perhaps to every individual, we live in a straight world that rewards coupling with the opposite sex and thus also rewards the denial of our more fluid erotic instincts. Feminists—both activists and therapists—built upon that insight, defanging some of Kinsey's and Freud's more sexist assumptions and popularizing the liberating elements of the work of Masters and Johnson.

Anne Koedt was one such popularizer. As a member of the Redstockings, an early and influential feminist group in New York, she helped develop the idea of consciousness-raising among women and organized the first abortion speak-outs. Koedt's most significant contribution to us all, though, was to debunk the fact that female pleasure is derived ideally from penetration. In 1968, she began analyzing the writings of Freud, a much-reviled figure for the ways he had dismissed women's complaints of dissatisfaction and abuse as psychological delusions. Koedt also studied the work of Masters and Johnson (published in 1966) whose examination of human sexual response asserted that the female orgasm originated in the clitoris and that women were, by and large, multi-orgasmic. (Freud had stated that clitoral orgasms existed but were only immature, and that getting pleasure from the clitoris was emulating masculine sexuality. Evolved women, according to Freud, had "vaginal orgasms.") In a few brisk paragraphs and one title that summed it all up—"The Myth of the Vaginal Orgasm"—Koedt's essay reaffirmed Masters and Johnson's "finding." Furthermore, she asserts women's *right* to have orgasms and concludes that there is no such thing as a frigid female, just inept male partners. (A point demonstrated about Kinsey, himself, in the 2004 movie, in which he is depicted as having been sexually inept early in his marriage. Kinsey and his wife sought marital counseling and that humility presaged his openness to human fumbling in his sexuality studies.) At the time of Koedt's article, when feminism was new and the media was hungry for their next bold statement, the work of do-it-yourself debunkers such as Koedt traveled fast and far.

Bisexuality, so clearly a major component in human sexuality, was studied again and again—so why does being bisexual remain denied or diminished? In the beginning was the word, and when the word is *bisexual*, you are already screwed. Or, as writer Jenny Weiss put it in *Girlfriends* magazine, "Of all the words for bisexual, the worst is probably bisexual." As a label, *bisexual* sounds pathological, academic, and a little embarrassed—like the identities "stay-at-home mom" and "runner-up." The synonyms that have been coined are far from positive—*fence-sitter, waffler, heartbreaker, disease vector.* The only one that can be construed as complimentary (or at least useful) is AC/DC—which is, after all, an adapter. Meanwhile, the one jaunty nickname, *bi*, sounds sort of half-assed, since *het* isn't used, nor is *homo* by any one other than Archie Bunker and modern-day fag bashers. *Lesbian, gay,* and *straight* are all more substantial terms. They have gravitas.

The term *bisexual* has ended up as the ugly stepchild of *sexuality*, both in name and meaning. Its fate is symptomatic of the bisexual's own lot in life: to be as common as can be, but unacknowledged. The term *lesbian* is derived from the Greek isle of Lesbos, in the northeastern Aegean Sea, where the lyric poet Sappho lived and wrote of her many female liaisons. But Sappho had male lovers as well, so to be accurate, not just *lesbian* (first coined in 1591) but the adjective or noun *Sapphic* should describe bisexuals. The ancient Roman poet Catullus writes of "Lesbia," that she is a woman with so much power over him that he is destroyed.[12] It is safe to assume that Lesbia had that power not as a woman who lived on a separatist commune, but as a woman who engaged with men but was not subservient to them.

Many people who might feasibly be described as bisexual do not choose to describe themselves that way. Not just because it sounds clinical or compromised, but because it sounds limiting. "Unlabelled experience can be strong stuff," writes Elise Mattheson, a self-identified bi from Minneapolis, on her Web site. The zine-maker Sabrina Margarita Alcantara-Tan, who is married and "queer," insists on the term *omnisexual* to indicate her sexuality. She is attracted to transgendered people and gay men, too, and for her, *bisexuality*, as it is currently understood, doesn't convey that scope.[13] Alcantara-Tan's verve in using a more self-made term is appealing. After all, even *lesbian* is a term made up by male sexologists, not women involved in same-sex relationships, according to the historian Lillian Faderman, who traced the history of women's romantic relationships in her book *Odd Girls and Twilight Lovers*. And then there are bisexuals such as Anne Heche, who "fall in love with a person," as she told Barbara Walters, and "don't put a label on it." Or the once-married Sapphic folkie Ani DiFranco, who famously sings, "I've got no criteria for sex or race / I just want to hear your voice / I just want to see your face."

The word *bisexual* makes me cringe at times, but saying I'm heterosexual or a lesbian feels inaccurate—regardless of who I am in a relationship with. So, cringing all the while, I use the label. Because of my relationship to the term *feminist*, I have learned that cringing is often a sign of unfinished political business: the label *bi* sounds bad because, at least in some ways, bisexuals are an unliberated, invisible, and disparaged social group.

For many, though, finding a word such as *bisexuality* is at least a start toward being seen and laying claim to an identity. "I can't categorize myself as just being a lesbian; it doesn't tell the whole story," says Natalie, one of the interviewees in *The Bisexual Spouse*, a 1989 book featuring six compelling case studies of spouses who had drives toward same-sex relationships. "And I've never considered myself to be a straight heterosexual either." Natalie's history is dialectic, a constant conversation between her relationships with men and those with women. The way that our culture has developed, if you take a bisexual woman and remove her life story from the picture, her identity suddenly makes no sense. It appears aberrant or a phase. In her thorough treatise on bisexuality, *Vice Versa: Bisexuality and the Eroticism of Everyday Life*, the Harvard English professor Marjorie Garber underscores the importance of storytelling in understanding bisexuality. She describes Tiresias—the "seer" in classic Greek texts. Tiresias had been both male and female at different times, and had "heterosexual" sex as a woman and as a man. "Tiresias mark[s] the place of a story rather than a body," writes Garber. "It is not any one state or stage of life but the whole life, the whole life 'story.' " Bisexuality, then, is a label that alludes to a life of changes and complexity in the most positive sense. It doesn't imply abnormal flux as opposed to normal fixed identity, but rather a human being's singular physical and emotional evolution.

As a culture, however, we seem to recognize only two homes for love and sex: gay and straight. The general presumption is that the vast majority of people are privileged to be straight, while a proud, growing minority is gay. Barbara Ehrenreich refers to this as the "gay-as-ethnic-group" approach to sexuality. In her May 1993 column in *Time* magazine, she noted that reducing sexuality to simply gay and straight:

> denies the true plasticity of human sexuality and, in so doing, helps heterosexuals evade that which they really fear. And what heterosexuals really fear is not that "they"—an alien subgroup with perverse tastes in bedfellows—are getting an undue share of power and attention, but that "they" might well be us.

Is this fear one of the reasons we regard the feminist woman who identifies as bisexual and loves Ani DiFranco as a cliché and a joke? "Lesbian Identity Ends Abruptly Mid-Junior Year" reads a January 31, 2002, cover story in the satirical weekly *The Onion*. "If it's true," the story has the "Campus Womyn's Caucus Chairwoman, age 20," saying, "that would imply that there is some aspect of collegiate revolutionary Marxist-feminist lesbian identity that is, in some way, less than completely genuine." Such a woman is actually straight and as a lesbian is merely in a disingenuous, self-serving, and for-the-boys-to-watch "phase." If she's not doing it for craven political gain, perhaps she's experimenting. In any case, she's a LUG, a "lesbian until graduation," when it's time to put down childish things, such as sleeping with the big lesbian on campus, and get thee to law school. Or she's just being "wild." My friend Marianne and I used to call that "see my new tattoo" bisexuality, meaning it's the safe appropriation of a signifier that once meant you were outside of society, but that now just means that you are under thirty. Emily Kramer, the (then) twenty-four-year-old cofounder of Cake, a New York–based social event that focuses on women's sexuality, told me a few years back that "at Andover [her prep school], all the cool, pretty girls made out with each other." Emily, who pretty much has always had a boyfriend, smooched the girls herself, but "it had more to do with defining myself as rebellious and not easy to pin down."

When bisexuality is not a "put-on" for an otherwise straight girl, like a Wonderbra or an ankle tattoo, then she's considered by many to be a dyke in denial. I once played Clue with several lesbian-feminist musicians and their friends while waiting out a snow storm in Durham, North Carolina, and the *B* word came up. "That was back when I used to say I was bisexual," said Melissa York, the drummer for punk bands such as Team Dresch and The Butchies, referring to an earlier time. Every other woman in the room nodded her head, indicating that she, too, remembered when she was less evolved in her sense of being gay and felt okay only to come out as bi. When queer-identified women and men marry people of the opposite sex—as Sabrina Margarita Alcantara-Tan, creator of *Bamboo Girl*, did in 1999—they are often seen as "actually" straight. The equally pathetic scenario is if they are thought to be "actually" gay but too cowed by internalized homophobia and convention to live honestly. Remember when we thought Tom and Nicole were beards for each other? I've heard the same about Hugh Grant and Liz Hurley and many other couples I won't mention, who are more believable than those above.

While feminists have pioneered sexual freedom, there is a way in which a bisexual feminist is sort of annoying, like a Republican feminist. When Meg Daly, the editor of the 1996 anthology *Surface Tension: Love, Sex, and Politics Between Lesbians and Straight Women*, got her first girlfriend, she identified as lesbian, deciding that her teen sex life with guys had been mostly exploitative of her and could thus be ignored as preconsciousness. "If there had been an option of bisexuality when I was coming out in the early nineties, I don't know what I would have thought of it," Meg told me. "I distinctly remember getting negative messages about bisexuals in the gay community once I moved to New York." When she started dating a man several years later, the fact that bisexuality wasn't a legitimate option left her feeling "identityless." "I tried to find a bisexual community in Portland," she recalled, "but it's not like finding the gay community. The groups that organize around the label *bisexuality* here are actually swingers or polyamorists"—she pauses—"and that just wasn't what I was going for." Daly's life has continued to be bisexual, in spite of the lack of community. In 2003, she was in her early thirties, the senior editor of *Just Out*, a queer paper in Portland, and was engaged to be married to a man—and just in time for gay marriage lawsuits in Oregon.

By 2004, she had gotten cold feet. When last we spoke she had a girlfriend and had relocated to the Bay Area.

In 2001, Ellen DeGeneres had the following exchange with a *New York Times Magazine* writer. The thread was about the dearth of openly lesbian couples in Hollywood for her to regard as models when she was coming out. "I don't regret [coming out in such a grand way with Anne Heche] . . . I'm glad there was a [famous lesbian] couple for a while, when there hadn't been one before," Ellen said. "Or since," the writer seconded. "But," Ellen said, "it turned out we weren't a gay couple either." She may have been splitting hairs and would identify Heche as bisexual, but my instinct is that Ellen meant that her former love was "really" straight.

Meanwhile, *Bust*, the magazine "for women with something to get off their chests," and the best example of third-wave sensibility in glossy print, alluded to a 2001 reader survey in which a "huge" percentage of younger women reported being bisexual or lesbian. The writer, *Bust's* very stylish, straight art director, Laurie Henzel, commented suggestively during an interview she was conducting, "I wonder about [whether they are really bi or gay]." Her interview subject, the filmmaker John Waters, responded with similar suspicion, albeit stated more colorfully: "I know! Because they aren't! Let's be real here—you can't fake eatin' pussy. That's putting it rudely, but you can make out for your boyfriend to turn him on . . . but actually, to be gay, you have to do things that are tough to fake if you really aren't at least bisexual." Reading his words, I pondered whether it was true that there were things you couldn't fake. I thought of the first five years I gave blow jobs, during which I had one mantra: *Don't gag! Don't gag! Okay, now just swallow . . . don't throw up! Don't throw up!*

In the face of the jokes and the disbelief in bisexual women's existence and the fact that very few people use the term *bisexual* to describe themselves and the assumption that you'd have to be pretty hardcore to go down on a woman is the plain fact that many, many women of my generation and those older and younger, while not identifying as lesbian, choose to have sexual and romantic relationships with other women. And these women often end up married, or were once married, or went on to have a boyfriend, or had only girlfriends but simply still felt attracted to men in emotional and sexual ways, too. When you consider how many of these women looked both ways, it seems clear that bisexuality is, in fact, ubiquitous.

The cover of *The Bisexual Spouse* asserts that "there are 25 million bisexual spouses in this country."[14] Meanwhile, the fact that "being bisexual automatically doubles your chance of a date on a Saturday night," as Woody Allen joked, is played out at some matchmaking services. At Spring Street, the successful personals arm of Nerve.com, all those looking for love are asked to specify whether it is a man, a woman, or either that they seek. Thirty-five percent of women in the Nerve.com system are seeking women or either—which corresponds, incidentally, with the percentage of women who reported bisexual experience in the Kinsey interviews—leaving only 65 percent who are full-on straight. A full 19 percent of the women say "either," which is 3 percent more than say they want only women.

Twenty-five percent of those "either" women are ages eighteen to twenty-four, and the percentage of women who want "either" goes up markedly the younger the woman. In my estimation, this is due to the fact that younger women are the daughters of both an active gay rights revolution and of second-wave feminism. They feel more freedom to have same-sex relationships without risk and harbor high expectations of equality in relationships. In my social group alone, more than half of the women either consider themselves bisexual or have conducted their love lives that way. Even my sister (who is straight but spent most of her teen years in the bathroom with her best friend doing god knows what) has had a blush-provoking crush on a go-go dancer and zine writer named Christine Doza. My former colleague Sandy's first love was her junior high best friend, with whom she knew mysterious passion on the shag rug after school. Shortly after the girl broke up with her, Sandy went on a family trip to Mexico, where older cousins tried to transform her from a gawky teen with braces, bushy hair, and defeated posture into a hot *mamacita*. No one knew that her dejectedness wasn't just a thirteen-year-old's being awkward—she was brokenhearted. A woman whom I met while I was on a date with Steven but who went on to pursue me with flowers and other gallantries dated women exclusively until her twenty-sixth year, at which point she started dating men exclusively. She's now married and refers to being with women as like living in London: "I want to really *be* in America," she says now, "but I will always love and miss London. It's wonderful to visit London." Anyone reading this book could possibly take her own inventory of her friends and come up with a paragraph just as full of acquaintances who have "looked both ways."

I had my first glimpse of a "joking" expression of bisexuality at Fargo South High, when the popular—and, it goes without saying, "straight"—guys, would occasionally pretend that they were rear-mounting one another as we loitered in the Commons between class bells. Their horseplay was meant to be both a dismissal of gay or anal sex and also proof that they were so straight that they could razz each other in that way. My younger sister remembers that the skater boys from South High would jerk off together on the half-pipe—a masturbat-a-thon of sorts. I remember the wooden paddles at college that fraternities gave to (and applied to) new brothers each winter, part of some traditional butt-spanking ritual. Those sorts of quasi-sexual single-sex activities are ingrained in the culture of American boys coming of age. I have to admit, until recently I had never contemplated what these boys got from these activities. Now it seems likely to me that they were able to bond in a way that enhanced their sense of power as a group— and, clearly, they got off a bit on this socially acceptable spanking.

Women don't often conduct circle jerks (although seventies feminists did pioneer orgasm workshops), and our coming-of-age rituals aren't the stuff of hundreds of movies (from *Summer of '42* to *American Pie*) or TV shows (*The Wonder Years* to *Dawson's Creek*). Taking that one step further, among the reasons the legitimacy of bisexual women is so in dispute is the fact that we haven't put good enough descriptions or images out in the world yet of who and what we are. This is a version of the problem Ellen DeGeneres alludes to when she speaks about the dearth of out lesbians in Hollywood as role models. As for bisexuals, without any other bisexuals (besides Elton John) to point to in mainstream culture, without any visible presence, it's easy to think that we're in denial. It's easy to write off a three-year relationship during which Anne bought a house with Ellen and called her "my wife" ad nauseum as just a phase. In a critical way, people's sexuality is viewed not by who they are but by which gender they sleep with at the present moment—as if there is no heart, no core, to *their* human sexuality.

There are analogies to corelessness in other groups, such as transgendered people (see Ariel Levy's discussion of tranny boys' machismo—she interprets it as women simply copying sexist male behavior—in her polemic *Female Chauvinist Pigs*) or biracial people. For example, the third-wave writer Rebecca Walker was supposed to be a manifestation of integration—her mother, Alice, southern black; her father, Mel Leventhal, East Coast Jew. Her parents came together as the civil rights movement was cresting and had biracial love child Rebecca in 1969. Then the seventies happened—with feminism and black power and separatism, leaving Rebecca to be the "black-white Jewish" kid shuffled from one broken home to another. With her mother, she was never seen as Jewish. Spending time in Westchester with her father, who had remarried a white woman with whom he had two younger children, Rebecca wasn't even assumed to be part of the family. In fact, she was often mistaken for the nanny. Never—or rarely—was she seen as her integrated whole self.

Walker herself has had male and female lovers, among them the bisexual single mother and singer-songwriter Meshell Ndegeocello. Walker worked for several years on a never-published anthology of bisexual writing called *Having Our Cake*, but it is in her memoir, *Black, White, and Jewish*, that she organically and unselfconsciously incorporates attraction to her childhood girlfriends and her burgeoning sense of heterosexuality. Her attractions are presented as natural—full-fledged—and don't create for Walker the same lack of visibility that race and culture do (which is probably why she didn't need to title the book *Black, White, Jewish, Straight, and Gay*). Her mother, too, has had male and female lovers, so perhaps Walker's confidence is enhanced by having plural sexuality be so familiar. Walker's non-neurotic stance is atypical in writing on the subject—but she's not alone; I see a blithely actualized bisexuality in Jonathan Franzen's character Denise, and in many of the women I interviewed for this book.

With the *Bust* example I suggested that feminists can be resistant to the idea that many women are bisexual, but women's liberationists are also the most sensitive describers of bisexuality. Feminist scholars and activists have done what they can to characterize women's sexuality accurately, and to disarm what was once considered threatening as being normal, whether it is masturbation or dissatisfaction with homemaking. Still, by and large, men have described sexuality first and most famously—and if we are talking about "experts," they are white men and quite frequently Austrian or German. These men wanted to know the "truth" about sexuality and its riddles, to be sure, but they were also hampered by the sexist and heterosexist assumptions of whatever time in which they lived and the limitations of their privilege.

This sad fact goes back to ancient Greece. We know Socrates, Plato, and friends thought the ideal was having a wife for the home, peers for intellectual stimulation, and nubile boys on the side—but what were the women doing during that time? In Aristophanes' play *Lysistrata*, the women decide to go on a sex strike to get their husbands to end the war between Athens and Sparta ("Making War? Then You Don't Get to Make Love" could have been their slogan). The ringleader, Lysistrata, exhorts the women of Sparta to prepare to stop putting out. In a plot twist long regarded as illogical by (I'm assuming male) scholars, the women don't retreat to their homes for the strike—they storm the Acropolis and hole up there. Of course, a strike in isolation wouldn't have worked. Women have a totally different sense of possibility when they are together in groups, which is why women organizing women is smartly seen as threatening. I can easily imagine that the Athenian women egged one another on, did consciousness-raising, drank wine, and danced with their togas off.

In fact, at each burst of women taking power in history, you can find a parallel spike of women falling for one another. Forget ancient Greece, look at the women who created and sang the blues in the early twentieth century. Bessie Smith and Billie Holiday were among the women who took female and male lovers as they toured the country. Witness the groups of white women during the Second World War who left the isolation of the home and went out to the factories. They finally had purpose other than home-making and were no longer isolated. Granted, they went back into the home when the men returned from the war, but they'd had a taste of other options, and their daughters saw the gleam in their mothers' eyes as well as the unfairness of their lives. Those daughters went on to be seventies feminists who left the confines of their homes (where they might rebel slightly, might be petulant, might take tranquilizers or have a martini at noon) and became the generation that created abortion rights, Title IX, feminist health movements, "womyn's" music, and battered women's shelters. For her compatriots, Jane Addams and the entire early-twentieth-century settlement house movement was an exercise in avoiding strangling female roles—and those female reformists fell in love with one another, too. Jane Addams had several female companions throughout her life, and there is ample evidence that they were what we now refer to as "partners."[15] Across the Atlantic, the feminist writers Simone de Beauvoir, Anaïs Nin, and Colette all had female and male lovers.

Sex (at least acknowledged sex) wasn't always part of the picture of women loving women. In fact, consciousness about sex coincided with the pathologizing of women being with women. During Victorian times, there were same-sex "romantic friendships," lauded by men in their writing, that held to the platonic ideals of love unsullied by sex—and thus were under the radar of heterosexuality. By the fin de siècle, making love was decidedly in the picture, accompanied by the terms *invert*, *lesbian*, and *degenerate*. Writings on same-sex attraction cropped up around the turn of the nineteenth century. The timing was not coincidental. The late 1800s were a time of feminist and abolitionist upheaval. White women were questioning why they didn't have a voice in the one way it mattered in a democracy—the vote. Many women asserted the immorality of "owning" another human being, whether as slave or that unpaid worker known as wife. Women of color—immigrant as well as African American women—identified injustices against themselves, too: In particular, how men's justification for denying them the vote often hinged on assumptions that women didn't do hard manual labor and were "protected" by men, whereas many poor women and women of color couldn't live an idealized feminine life. "Nobody ever helps me into carriages, or over mud-puddles, or gives me any best place! And ain't I a woman?" Sojourner Truth is said to have asked, dashing the weaker-sex argument in twenty-one words at a women's rights convention in the mid-1800s. Out at meetings for women's suffrage or abolition, women suddenly got to see one another. They learned they could have creative and intellectual partnerships like the one that Thomas Jefferson had with James Madison, or Ralph Waldo Emerson had with Bronson Alcott. Elizabeth Cady Stanton and Susan B. Anthony aligned with each other to create a formidable partnership: "In thought and sympathy we were one," wrote Stanton of their creative union. "And in the division of labor we exactly complemented each other." They weren't lovers, but she could have been describing the perfect feminist marriage.

By the time women actually got the vote twenty years into the twentieth century, bisexuality was apparent in many of the cultural icons of the time. Women were taking on new roles and more "masculine" looks, such as that of the liberated flapper. Cheeky and boyish, the early-twentieth-century woman smoked and probably had sex; she could vote, and she didn't have to attend earnest suffrage parades or wear silly bloomers to make a point as previous generations had. Then there were the aforementioned bisexual arbiters of the Jazz Age, such as Billie Holiday and Ma Rainey, who anticipated rock 'n' roll and civil rights by making white people come to them. And there were the artists. The women of the Harlem Renaissance, the bohemians of Greenwich Village such as Djuna Barnes and HD (or Hilda Doolittle, whom Freud vaunted as a "perfect bi"), and the art and writing of Bloomsbury members such as Virginia Woolf and Lytton Strachey, for whom bisexuality was the order of the day. The great Coco Chanel, who influenced chic more than any other designer, had male and female lovers, too. So did the poet Elizabeth Bishop and the novelist Iris Murdoch. Looking both ways seemed to give creative energy to female artists and writers. Perhaps it was the strength of being surrounded by people regarded by sexist society as having the same value that enabled these women to compete directly with men, rather than be cowed by them. Perhaps it was standing both within convention and outside of it that contributed to these women's unique visions of the world.

Even women famous for having legions of male suitors were of the Sapphic persuasion—at least part of the time. The poet Edna St. Vincent Millay—a beauty and breathtaking celebrity—had been a major rake at Vassar, seducing all the girls, and was reputed to be the model for Lakey, Mary McCarthy's naughty lesbian in her 1954 novel, *The Group*. Millay, who was called "Vincent" in college, eventually married but continued to have no end of male lovers and admirers. "My candle burns at both ends / It will not last the night / But ah, my foes and oh my friends / It gives a lovely light"—her most famous verse reads a bit differently when we know that she had both male and female paramours lining up outside her door.

Women achieving the vote in 1920 is often cited as the historical designation of the end of the first wave of feminism. The twenties are often seen as a time of decadence (rather than revolution) for the newly liberated women.

The behavior engaged in then prompted older suffragists to scoff (so what if the gals could smoke?), in the same way that some seventies pioneers now roll their eyes at the notion that younger women use their increased freedom to get Brazilian bikini waxes.

The characterization, though, is not quite fair. The first step of any revolution is the political gesture, the articulation of the right itself. Elizabeth Cady Stanton did that when she revamped the Declaration of Independence to include women (The Declaration of Sentiments), adding that females shall have the right to vote. The next step has to do with believing in one's freedom. The personal consciousness change is much messier. After all, it is its permeation into and then transformation of the mainstream culture that makes any ideology more than just rhetoric. Thus, women's right to vote was followed by a decade in which women bobbed their hair, reached for a Lucky instead of a sweet, and wore fun dresses in which they could dance. They created art and music and writing that did as much to instigate freedom's spirit in individual lives as laws can to actualize freedoms formally. Women of the time could conduct themselves as men did, and manifest in this sense of entitlement were the greater rights they had over previous generations.

Let's return to Freud and the social context for his arrival. It was just before the vote, women were getting birth control from Margaret Sanger and others, and Emma Goldman was making headlines as an anarchist, labor organizer, and free-love activist. This birth control revolution affirmed that sex was for pleasure, not just procreation, and just then, Freud's ideas entered and changed the culture on a grand scale at the time. Just as two million men were shipped away to fight the First World War, people began realizing that they had all manner of repressed desires itching to emerge in one neurosis or another. The historian Lillian Faderman describes the 1920s as a time "when many women were giving themselves permission to explore sex between women."[16] She cites a sociologist of the time who studied 2,200 women and found that more than 1,100 of them had "intense" relationships with other women and half of those 1,100 admitted that the relationship was sexual either in tone or act. But these weren't lesbians: "They frequently saw the relationship as . . . isolated . . . and they expected eventually to marry and live as heterosexuals." Faderman calls this era one of lesbian chic (a phrase that popped up again in the early 1990s and that I'm sure we haven't seen the last of)—meaning that otherwise straight women believed that the times allowed some "experimentation," and that expressing one's attraction to women held some currency. The cultural mandate to marry was much stronger, however, and even if bisexual attraction wasn't a phase for these women, it had to be treated as one.

While Kinsey or the *Sex in America* researchers would argue that there are social conventions that convince us not to deviate from the straight and narrow, there were increasingly other, equally compelling social benefits to looking both ways, ones pointed to by feminism. Feminists used the tool of consciousness-raising to identify and analyze the outside forces that kept women down. At a certain point, though, some feminists believed they had hit a wall with consciousness. Old patterns die hard, and those early feminists turned to psychoanalytic theory in an attempt to understand why it was so difficult to make personal changes. What they found useful was the idea that we all have an unconscious. "This belief in the unconscious forced us to really engage with Freud," Laura Kogel, a New York–based therapist told me. "And we learned that we could build on his insights." She continued:

Freud had one picture of drives—as overwhelming, unconscious urges toward sex or aggression that defined our relationships with our parents, friends, and lovers. Women, who didn't express sexuality or aggression in the same ways as men, appeared dysfunctional within that portrait. Slowly over time, feminist therapists changed how we think about the unconscious in ways that complement and improve upon Freud. At this point, what we try to relate in psychoanalysis is that the unconscious is populated with relationships—relationships that involve sexuality and aggression and self worth. It is the relationship that contains the drives, rather than the drives forming the relationships, as Freud assumed.

Relational psychologists such as Carol Gilligan discovered that the human need to give and receive love and care is a profound "drive." In order to preserve their connections to others, women can suppress their own desires. The prevailing Freudian/sexist perception was that women do this out of weakness and pathology. Gilligan and others such as Jean Baker Miller found that women often do it to stay in a relationship with the people they need. The work of feminist therapists used the insights of Freud while removing his sexist blinders. In *Understanding Women*, the feminist therapists Luise Eichenbaum and Susie Orbach note,

> Had Freud written at a different time, he might have developed a theory according to which the main focus in the psychological development of both boys and girls was on the mother's breasts, the hopes that a girl would have that she would then grow up to have a mother's body, and the boy's feelings of inadequacy because he did not possess those marvelous breasts. After all, babies have far more contact with breasts than with penises.

Feminism is the belief that women are as valuable as men. A same-sex environment is one way to activate that idea for women—taking it from rhetoric to something women really feel. When I got to *Ms.*, I felt alive in the conversations about feminism, in love with the intimacy, and freed up from worrying about how men perceived me (something I'd wasted too much time doing). But it wasn't simply the lack of men around (except for Jimmy, the mailroom guy) that forced us off the otherwise powerful script of heterosexuality. It was also that women often have tremendous value in these self-chosen all-female spaces. At my grandmother's retirement village, for instance, she lives in what is essentially a girls' dormitory. Because men tend to die younger, Waterford is filled with widows—silver-haired, dashing, lively women who love to hug and kiss one another in greeting, creating an atmosphere of support and affection and companionship. In the main room—a huge parlor with Ethan Allen furnishings and a gas fireplace and fake logs—are displayed photos of Grandma and her clique: nearly all women at the Valentine's Day dinner; nearly all women for the St. Paddy's Day party. Only one or two husband-wife couples appear in the photos. The rest is a sea of women freed up to love one another's company. They are not bisexual, but I feel confident saying that many are certainly engaged in romantic friendships in the robust Victorian sense.

Rosie the Riveter and the heroines of *Lysistrata* and all the girls at the Ani DiFranco concert aren't just about politics and negotiations to confront our oppression. Looking both ways is also about crazy, overwhelming, cue-the-orchestra *love.* "Perhaps it is time to acknowledge that the potential to fall in love with a person of the same sex," wrote Barbara Ehrenreich in that *Time* op-ed in 1993, "is widespread among otherwise perfectly conventional people." Looking both ways is also about hot, messy, cue-the-Led-Zeppelin-record sex. "We were women taking power," Alix Kates Shulman said to me about her second-wave sisters falling for one another, "and that is always very sexy." Henry Kissinger, an unhandsome wonk with many a beauty on his arm in his day, was right: power is the ultimate aphrodisiac.

CHAPTER 3

THE WOMAN-IDENTIFIED WOMAN: BISEXUALITY AND THE SECOND WAVE

Some folks think Sappho was a little "touched" / Well I think Sappho just loved that touch we all love so much.

—Teresa Trull, "Woman-loving Women," from the Olivia release *Lesbian Concentrate*, 1977

I would guess that 98 percent of WLMers [women's liberation movement] were bi, at least in the sense that we all started out with the usual exclusively het behaviors. Only after 1970 did most of us "go gay." One's former relationships with men continued in a whole lot of cases.

—Author and second-waver Naomi Weisstein, in an e-mail to me, 2002

An unforeseen advantage to moving to New York after college was that I could just pick up the phone and call the women I had read about in *Daring to Be Bad*, Alice Echols's truly fascinating history of seventies feminists. After all, I now lived in town with them. In my twenties, I had tea or lunch or a drink or at least a phone call with anyone I could track down—from Ellen Willis to Shulamith Firestone (the J. D. Salinger of feminism—brilliant, eccentric, rarely seen)—and some of these cold calls turned into friendships. Over the years, I learned even more about the gossip, mistakes, and triumphs of the radical women behind the second wave—and I learned about their love lives. Many of these putatively straight women had fallen for movement sisters back in the day—for instance, Karen Durbin, now the film critic for *Elle*, has mainly dated men but had an affair with another feminist whom she calls "one of the great loves" of her life; the married writer Joan K. Peters (author of *When Mothers Work: Loving Our Children Without Sacrificing Ourselves*) was once in love with the novelist Blanche McCrary Boyd. Eve Ensler, Byllye Avery, Audre Lorde, Robin Morgan . . . the list was long. Many

second-wavers didn't fall for women, of course (Gloria
Steinem, Shulamith Firestone, Susan Brownmiller, Ellen
Willis, to name a few), but it was surprising to me how
many had—and how many who I thought were lesbians had
been married or were otherwise romantically involved with
men, including Alice Walker and Jan Clausen.

Few of the second-wave women I met or read about referred to themselves as bisexual. For most, having female
lovers had felt natural, an outgrowth of the rising esteem
they were feeling for women and the excitement of changing one's own culture so rapidly. Bisexuality, though, remained veiled. Analyzing sexual politics had animated their
movement, and understanding how to deal with a woman
who enjoyed both heterosexual privilege *and* the egalitarian
privilege of love among sister equals was beyond the theories of the time. Still, it was the women who looked both
ways who tended to define and push the women's movement in the seventies, whether or not they identified themselves as bisexual.

On August 31, 1970, twenty-nine-year-old artist Kate
Millett was featured on the cover of *Time* as the star
spokesperson for the rapidly crescendoing, two-year-old
"women's lib" movement. Her Ph.D. thesis from Columbia
University had been released in 1970 as *Sexual Politics*, a
fresh bestseller of radical feminism. Hungry for stories
about the new controversial "libbers," the press leapt on the
artist and activist, virtually staking out the Bowery loft
she occupied with her then-husband, the sculptor Fumio
Yoshimura. The contemporary feminist movement had
been, up until that point, identified most closely with
women such as Betty Friedan—ambitious working women
who were typically married, suburban, and quite often
mothers. Those women were seeking access to male do-
mains such as electoral politics, high-paying jobs, and male-
only establishments—the Oak Room in the Plaza Hotel,

the firehouse, and the Senate. The new feminists came out of other radical movements—civil rights, Students for a Democratic Society, or the peace movement—and were generally younger and more on the "fringe." These women were more threatening, as they were declaring war on the bedroom (and all areas of intimate life) as well as on the boardroom—not to mention critiquing the adoption of male roles and values advocated by Friedan. Most media coverage of the new radicals tended to be written by men and was cynical and undermining of their cause. The *Time* piece stood out not so much for being laudatory as for merely acknowledging that something big was happening.

Three months later, on December 14, 1970, *Time* ran a much smaller piece on Millett. This piece was an exposé, reporting a "damaging" fact about the star feminist. "Ironically," the piece began, "Kate Millett herself contributed to the growing cynicism about the [women's] movement by acknowledging at a recent meeting that she was bisexual." The *Time* writer went on to surmise that "the disclosure is bound to discredit her as a spokeswoman for her cause, cast further doubts on her theories, and reinforce the views of those skeptics who routinely dismiss liberationists as lesbians."[17]

Millett was successfully discredited, in a way, and her treatment in the media pointed to intersecting tensions. The women's movement was just one of several civil rights mobilizations crashing through American culture; another crucial movement was gay liberation, which shared with feminism an investment in abolishing female/male stereotypes and mandates for feminine behavior. However, while women's lives had changed quite a bit in the early 1960s (evidenced as much by Helen Gurley Brown's bestseller *Sex and the Single Girl* as by Betty Friedan's *The Feminine Mystique*), lesbianism and bisexuality were still in their pre-1950s (and earlier) incarnations. That is, they were considered deviant, shameful, and unnatural. Gurley Brown's revelation that "nice girls do" aside, women's sexuality was still so misunderstood and invisible that there weren't even laws barring women from having sex with one another. The sodomy statutes of most states were used only against gay men. This invisibility continues. The two major Supreme Court cases regarding queer sex—*Bowers v. Hardwick* (1986), and *Lawrence v. Texas* (2003)—both concerned sex between men. Nevertheless, overt romantic socializing among women was relegated to seedy mob-controlled bars and was subject to humiliating police raids. At the same time, *within* the movement of the second wave, there were polarizing debates about lesbianism. The most infamous episode was at the 1970 Second Congress to Unite Women: lesbians clad in T-shirts reading LAVENDER MENACE confronted Betty Friedan's use of that phrase to disparage the queer women who, Friedan thought, could derail the straight women's chances for integration into male, heterosexual spheres.

Meanwhile, radical feminists had their own debates about queer women, especially those who took on "male" behavior. "Lesbian is a label invented by the Man," the collective known as Radicalesbians wrote in 1970 in their manifesto *The Woman-Identified Woman*. The label is thrown "at any woman who dares to be his equal, who dares to challenge his prerogatives (including that of all women as part of the exchange medium among men), who dares to assert the primacy of her own needs."

The manifesto also derided as politically retrograde the emulating of masculine behavior by butch women. Joan Nestle, the creator of the Lesbian Herstory Archives and prominent second-wave activist, writes of that time: "I knew what I liked in bed and I pursued the butch women who welcomed my desire . . . I was queer and a fem, and a fem was not the same as being a woman." When Nestle learned of feminism, she was able to trade in her "deviant" status for the much better "oppressed" status—since men, straight *and* gay, oppressed her. But the trade-off meant denying part of herself and her former community because of the antagonism directed at butch lesbians. In *The Feminist Memoir Project,* Nestle recalls attending a feminist meeting, when two older butches with brush cuts—the kind of women whom she remembers from her earlier formative bar experiences— venture in. Later, in the bathroom, she hears younger, and newly lesbian, feminists gossip about them: "Did you see those two gray-haired women who just walked in? Why do they have to look like men? I hope they don't come back." They didn't, of course.[18]

Similar to Joan Nestle's experience, the second short film in HBO's remarkable *If These Walls Could Talk 2*, portrays a seventies hippie feminist who brings home an old-school butch she meets at a bar (played with nice credibility by Chloë Sevigny) and is chastised by her woman-identified, recently Sapphic co-op mates. Sevigny's character is made to feel foolish and devalued in her leather jacket and ducktail, despite the fact that she and the hippie chick, played by Michelle Williams, had great sex the night before. More than the sex, though, Williams's character really likes the butch woman. Since young, new feminists (and probably recently minted lesbians) of that day "hoped butches [wouldn't] come back," Williams's character is left without a way to accommodate her own desire, seeing it only as a vestige of her patriarchal conditioning.

In their quest for liberation, some feminists politicized sex almost to a fault. Another radical argument for looking to women in the 1970s underscored the political purity and courage of women who gave up the sexist privileges garnered by their association with men. Those women were known as "political lesbians." They might not have ever slept with a woman—indeed, they might have been straight— but they disavowed heterosexual identity and men.

Radical second-wave feminists pioneered the concept that one can choose one's sexuality depending on one's values, politics, and understanding of freedom. The "woman-identified woman," according to the Radicalesbians, privileged women over men at all times, including in matters of love and sex. A group founded by Ti-Grace Atkinson, simply named The Feminists, didn't allow more than a third of their members to be with a man. "The early women's liberation movement not only welcomed lesbians, it *created* them," wrote Naomi Weisstein, a scientist and founder of the Chicago Women's Liberation Rock Band and the Chicago Women's Liberation Union.[19]

> Despairing of our oppressive relationship with men, and understanding for the first time that our problems with men were systemic, i.e., not simply our own fault and not easily solved, we began to ask ourselves the question, "Why bother?" We began to question patriarchal imperatives that told us to stay away from sex with other women under threat of being considered "queer" or "sick" or—heaven forbid—"unable to get a man."

But Weisstein goes on to emphasize that it wasn't merely that men were not meeting women's liberationists' needs—or at least not changing fast enough—but also that these women's liberationists had fallen in love with each other. According to Weisstein:

> We early pioneers loved each other intensely, passionately, and without reservation. We faced difficult, frightening, often dangerous struggles . . . Those of us who stayed the course became inseparable, like soldiers in a long hard war. But, unlike ordinary soldiers in somebody else's war, we were volunteers in a revolutionary move-

ment whose business it was to break gender and culture boundaries and to loosen ancient codes.

The consciousness-raising movement of the time, coupled with a profound sense that one could squirm out of all of the tight shackles of femininity, dovetailed beautifully with looking toward women. Women weren't "coming out"; they were "coming in," to a movement—a separate world—that valued women sexually, emotionally, and intellectually. Who could resist that?

Other feminist luminaries drew from their same-sex relationships to shape influential theories. As for Millett, her high school relationship with a female classmate—a tryst that got young Kate kicked out of school—surely played some role in her ability to see through the "scheme that prevails in the area of sex," as she wrote in *Sexual Politics*, "[providing our] most fundamental concept of power." But it's likely that her relationships with men did, too. As indicated by the wording in the *Time* piece, Millett's bisexuality was misread as her lesbianism. It made sense that a resistant and macho media failed to grasp the full humanity of women's sexuality and desires; it was more surprising that the feminist movement failed to as well. Kate Millett, Alix Kates Shulman, Robin Morgan, Byllye Avery, Angela Davis, Alice Walker, Germaine Greer, Charlotte Bunch, and Audre Lorde were all iconic writers and activists of the second wave who had relationships with both women and men. Second-wave Brit wit Germaine Greer had a teenage love affair with a best friend and went on to be overachievingly heterosexual. Her affair is alluded to in several of her books, serving chiefly as an antidote to her fear and loathing of her mother's ultrafeminine wiles. What keeps Greer's books from tipping over into the morass of misogyny (always a profitable position, from a publishing point of view) is her loving and detailed depiction of women's bodies and what they are capable of. It's not hard for me to imagine that her schoolgirl affair informed the best of her feminist writing. How did she know so definitively that sex is not the same as reproduction? What made her title a chapter "Curves"? Patricia Ireland, a second-waver who was president of the National Organization for Women from 1991 to 2001, happily had both a husband and a longtime girlfriend. This fact thrills me but, sadly, it contributed to her losing her job in 2003 as the executive director of the Girl Scouts, when conservative groups such as the Traditional Values Coalition launched a homophobic letter campaign.

The fact is, second-wave women thought about looking both ways a lot, even though they rarely described their lives or insights as bisexual. Instead, they were woman-identified women or political lesbians (gay in the streets if not in the sheets, to paraphrase rock critic Ann Powers) and, for some, these relationships remained private and unlabeled. For many women who identified as lesbians, relegating their former marriages or even their male prom dates to the dustbin of prefeminist history, there was no space for discussion of those old relationships as anything other than inauthentic or subject to critique. There was no space for the person—or part of the person—who still felt attraction toward men. Moreover, their love relationships with women suffered the opposite fate. They were presumed to be de facto ideal. Complaints, boredom, and frustration were suppressed and seen as the problem of the individual dissatisfied woman. The role of frigid, unhappy, neurotic partner was one that women had just learned to debunk in their affairs with men—but now, to have to apply that raised consciousness to their relationships with women? It was too confusing, too new, and too dangerous to ponder.

Jan Clausen, a poet and part of the younger second wave, wrote the first feminist critique of lesbian relationships (from within) I ever saw. She was twenty-three in 1973 when she moved to New York. She recalls that by then the movement had already been "Balkanized" into the gay/straight split, the black/white split, and the "love *Ms.*"/ "think it's a CIA front" split. "There was a sense that the most important stuff had already happened," Clausen told me, but she walked right in to a very developed, nurturing community of lesbian-feminist writers:

> I belonged to a poetry group called Seven Women Poets. Most of the women in the group had been involved with men—I mean, one of them had been married and even had a child. Essentially, it was a lot of women who had led heterosexual lives at one time, and it was understood that we hadn't known any better. It wasn't the theoretical concept of attraction to men that was an anathema—but practically, it wasn't happening, and no one imagined that it could happen. My group was so defined by being committed to women that there was no room for anything else.

As Clausen's experience signals, the radical-feminist movement immediately changed the terms of the debate surrounding what used to be called "the woman question," in Communist and left circles. (In other words, how should male leaders deal with women in the new revolutionary society?) In the late sixties and early seventies, women knocked down that object role, asking questions right back of men and society. *Why does my husband get to relax with a martini and the paper while I fix dinner and then clean up? Why is abortion illegal given that more than a million women need the service each year? Why do I take his name? Why am I wearing a girdle and high heels to a baseball game? Why can I be fired if I don't sleep with my boss? Why isn't there daycare? Why don't I know how to have an orgasm?* The questions tackled every area of life, shattering assumptions about how men's and women's lives were to unfold. The novelist and second-wave feminist Alix Kates Shulman thought of them as the "burning questions." One other burning question was *Why bother with men?*

Alix Kates Shulman's second novel is called *Burning Questions*. In it, her character Zane IndiAnna grapples with sexual politics. As a college freshman, Shulman wrote an essay entitled "The Great Illusion." Its thesis was that because of our "modern American way of life, mate selection must result from intelligent analysis, rather than from romantic love, if successful marriage is to ensue." At eighteen, Shulman was the sharp-eyed observer of her mother, who gave up a career she loved (as a project designer for the WPA) and who had bought into the post–Second World War propaganda that said women should head back to the hearth now that the men were home. Shulman's much-adored father, a lawyer, treated his daughter like a brilliant and serious thinker ("as if I were a son," as Shulman puts it), and she learned to write at his elbow, watching him create his briefs. Shulman loved her mother's friends, especially the independent women she only later realized were lesbians.

As a young married beatnik in New York City, Shulman hung out in lesbian bars. "I was always around women who were attracted to women," she says. "That wasn't strange to me at all. It was just that I was heterosexual." Even later, she was a mother married to a guy who through no fault of his own—a victim of his time, perhaps, as much as she was— just didn't get it. At age thirty-six she was in Redstockings, one of the few mothers in the early radical-feminist group best known for pioneering consciousness-raising groups for women and inventing the pro-woman line. She protested the Miss America pageant in 1968 and 1969, helping to launch radical-feminist activism into American pop culture. Amid infidelities with various men during three marriages, Shulman also fell in love with three women, movement sisters all. But before examining her personal life, it's important to have a sense of Shulman's work, which describes the time and its shifts so well.

Sasha, the heroine of Alix Kates Shulman's first (and most famous) book, *Memoirs of an Ex-Prom Queen*, is clever and intellectual, plays chess, and reads Emerson (self-reliance makes a big impression on the young gal). She is also competitive with girlfriends for the title of most beautiful (aka prom queen), prone to messy affairs, and somewhat sexually liberated. Well, she has plenty of sex before marriage—twenty-six lovers in all, in fact—gets the clap, has an abortion, and is married to a pretentious intellectual and later a guy who, after the kids are born, proves quite sexist, philandering, and bitter. It's the late sixties. Sasha, like Shulman, is a child of the forties.

Memoirs was hailed by fellow feminist Kate Millett as the first novel of the women's liberation movement. In it, Sasha's moment of truth comes pages from the end of the book, when she has her hair cut off to recapture how she wore it when she was a teenager and was crowned queen of the prom. While the sixties' counterculture is growing Sasha is having babies, and suddenly she feels less than hip. Mr. John, her hairdresser, chops her locks without the panache needed to transform her into Mia Farrow, much less her seventeen-year-old self. Under a blasting hot dryer, sweating and leafing through women's magazines, Sasha begins to hallucinate, overwhelmed by all of the misogyny she's taken in over her lifetime. The magazines provide her with the "necessary connections between cause and effect that had eluded [her] in all of [her] study of philosophy."[20] She sees how women are written to and about and how those depictions have warped her. The hair (symbolizing naïve prom queen Sasha) can never be the same because Sasha is not the same. In that moment, too, she realizes that attempting to recapture her youth is to lose her wisdom and her feminist insight. Sasha arrives home feeling less attached to her looks than at any other point in the book or her life—and greets her husband, who freaks out at her bad haircut.

> "How could you do it?" he whispered.
> "Christ, Willy," I cried, "it's just *hair!* It'll grow in again!"
> But it was only out of habit that I reassured him, for I knew after it grew back in it wouldn't really be the same.

With that, Sasha calls her friend Roxanne, a single mom who is into women's liberation, and the book is over. The final hair scene—where you realize this is a radical break for Sasha, who no longer wants to go back to being a seventeen-year-old prom queen—is a kind of amalgam of Nora slamming the door as she leaves Torvald Helmer in Ibsen's *A Doll's House* and the climax of F. Scott Fitzgerald's "Bernice Bobs Her Hair." In "Bernice," a flapper-era woman is cheered on as she goes to cut her hair—and in the process says goodbye to the past and embraces modernity. Once the novelty wears off, she's ignored, left feeling exposed and abandoned, but "free."

Shulman's *Memoirs* is more about the pre-liberated woman than the feminist. Not incidentally, Sasha has no affairs with women. With Zane IndiAnna, the heroine of her 1978 novel *Burning Questions*, Shulman explores feminist ardor full on. Like Sasha and Shulman, Zane is smart, pretty, and curious, but she hits Sasha's moment of truth early on in the book, running into the women's liberation movement as it heats up New York in the late sixties. Zane, too, is married to a sexist guy who is otherwise fairly decent, but she falls in love with one of her "sisters," a woman named Faith, in her C-R (consciousness-raising) and action group and is immediately overcome by the revolutionary aspects of this love.

Woman and man, man and woman. From the most trivial kindness to the weightiest sacrifice; it was there, the burdensome consciousness of our sexes, carrying the import of millennia.

But with Faith, nothing at all was given. What did "woman's part" even mean between us? . . . If we had roles we'd have to invent them and choose the parts ourselves . . .

"Vive la différence," I said, running my fingers over her smooth, mysterious belly. Another astonishment. Faith was soft as a rose petal. Her body, so like mine, ought to have felt as familiar as a hand, and yet it was strange and wonderful to my touch, as mysterious as an insect's delicate wing. Her hair was long and silken, her hip curved like a teacup, her shoulder fit into my palm, she had no edges or angles or coarse fur or stubble.[21]

Zane and Faith fall in love just as the decade turns from the tumultuous but hopeful sixties to the compromised, heartbreaking seventies. Their idealistic love is climactic, but it foreshadows a hard decade, full of disappointments for these women's individual lives. Also, and more profoundly, it alludes to a hard decade for the women's movement. When we meet Zane again, in the late seventies, she's a teacher and lecturer, while Faith is out of the picture and living on a "women's farm." In the last chapter, Zane enumerates the things that have changed due to women's unfinished revolution, including the fact that relations between the sexes are better.

"It's so different nowadays that it's almost impossible for someone like you to comprehend," Shulman told me in an interview. "Growing up in the forties and fifties, the most important thing was to get a man, to get married, to get the best catch you can, and everything was a prelude to that. So, if you were going to be out with your girlfriends but then some guy asked you out on a date, everyone just assumed that you'd go out with the guy, of course, because they would have, too."

Life was sexist back then. Men had all the power and prestige and women were helpmates, power's little copilots—or, more likely, stewardesses, "thanking people" as former Pan Am stewardess Patricia Ireland once remarked, "as they take their garbage." "Okay, then suddenly here was the women's movement," continues Shulman.

> Here was a serious endeavor, really intimate bonding with other women over something that was so much more important than a date, or getting a man. In fact, getting a man was quickly revealed not only as not inevitable but perhaps not even desirable. That kind of intensity and intimacy was in many cases bound to erupt into the erotic—not experimentation, exactly, although there was that—but falling in love. So, when I put falling in love with a woman as a climax of the intense women's liberation phase of Zane's life, it seemed like a climax that was pretty widespread.

Feminism, which coincided with the burgeoning gay rights movement, had turned the whole assumption of compulsory heterosexuality on its ear through its exploration of gender. In fact, "Compulsory Heterosexuality and Lesbian Existence" is the title of a famous essay published in 1980 by second-wave poet and thinker Adrienne Rich. In it, she questions the universality or naturalness of heterosexuality and accepts the Freudian observation that the original bond for both men and women is to their mothers, pointing to lesbianism as most natural for women and heterosexual desire as most natural for men. Her essay has been widely critiqued for suggesting that there is any one natural sexuality, but at the time she was one of the only major intellectuals since Freud to assert that homosexuality was anything other than a problem. She is also notable for describing a continuum, like Kinsey's, of lesbian love—a continuum that begins with the intimacy of a mother nursing her daughter and ends with a nurturing, egalitarian love relationship between two women. While this theory eventually contributed to the stifling sterotype that lesbians only cuddle and nuzzle in bed, supporting each other and drinking chamomile tea, Rich was savvy to link same-sex love—so taboo, so unnatural!—with a role for women seen as unassailable: being a mother.

For Shulman, after two kids and a decade of marriage to a man who she felt resented her every attempt to be freer, here was a whole movement to support and encourage her independence and growth. Moreover, men were decidedly excluded from her feminist life, as the women's liberation movement did not permit men to attend meetings. "They could be auxiliaries," Shulman recalls. "We allowed them to run the daycare parts of our meetings or conferences. There were functions they could serve but, you know, let them make the coffee and take care of the children." And the movement was tremendously erotic and sexy because women were the smart ones, women held the power, women were central and at the ramparts, creating a revolution for themselves. Up until then, feminism had a dour, sexless image—hatchet-faced Susan B. Anthony or roly-poly mother of eight Elizabeth Cady Stanton. Sojourner Truth's (possibly apocryphal) baring her breasts to a roomful of men was an effort to prove she was a woman to her crude challengers, not a proto–Drew Barrymore move.

Still, "bisexuality was not a concept that had much currency, and there was a lot of contempt for both heterosexuality and for bisexuality," Shulman recalls, maybe more for bisexuality because it seemed like trying to get the privileges.

I fell in love with three different women. It was such a long time ago, I hope I get their order right. The first woman was a little older than I was and she had written a book that I admired a lot. She was a very difficult person, unfortunately. Once, we were driving somewhere and we had this great big fight about her driving—she was a mad driver and I couldn't stand being in the car with her. My husband at the time was a mad driver and I had two little children and I was sure he was going to kill them and that was one reason I wanted to leave him.

We only kissed a couple of times. We had this great kiss up in the window. I remember it was in my apartment, which was on Washington Square and I thought . . . I mean I was married, I had two kids and they were little. My husband would have taken the children from me. It felt like a very heavy thing. Unlike most of my friends at the time, who weren't married or didn't have kids, I was very protective of my children and there we were in front of the window and I thought, oh my god, what am I doing? I was endangering my whole life. It was always very clear to me that what came first was arranging my life in such a way that my children would be okay. And I was always horrified about the women who ran off and left their children, even if they ran off with other women. Rita Mae Brown, who was this tremendous flirt, used to flirt with me like crazy. She'd say, "When are you going to leave that husband and come off with me?" And I'd say, "Whenever you're ready to do half of the babysitting," and then we would laugh.

In those days, if you were a lesbian, if you ever brought a woman into the house or anything, you were an unfit mother.[22] There were many people who pioneered overturning those rules, but I wasn't one of them, nor would I have been. Too dangerous.

Margaret Fiedler was my second lover and was in many ways my best friend. [She died in 2005.] I never felt as intimate with anybody as I did with Margaret. Margaret was a completely free spirit, she had many lovers, she was a proto-hippie. And she was an amazing creature—a midwife, a mystic. Oh, exclusivity was never part of her life or her expectation of me. I met her because Barbara Seaman was having a party and thought that we would like each other. We looked across the room and *zing!* Enchantment. It was so amazing that I brought her home with me.

It was 1972. My then-husband was out of town, as he always was. The children adored her, and she adored them. And we just stayed up playing with the children and having the most fabulous time. We wanted to sleep together but, again, I was terrified. I don't remember if I was separated from my husband then or not. I may have been. I didn't want to put the children in the position of having to lie or testify or anything. I made her sleep on the top bunk in my son's room so that the children would know that she had slept in the "guest room."

In 1975, Shulman was teaching at Sagaris, a feminist freedom school/summer institute at Goddard College, in Vermont. The big names in women's liberation, including Margaret Fiedler, taught at one of two five-week summer sessions. The women who would attend the sessions ranged from welfare mothers to career academics.[23] In many ways, Sagaris was a microcosm of the women's liberation movement, and Shulman's experiences there bore some similarities to my own at *Ms.* magazine—especially in her perception of the place as a Sapphic hothouse.

I met my third love while teaching at Sagaris. Perhaps it was because those vibes were already in the air from Margaret having been there the session before (we overlapped a couple of days and made love)—or because they were generally in the air at Sagaris for the first session, it seemed that everybody there was a lesbian. I have no idea what proportion of people who came to Sagaris were already lesbians, but it was probably pretty low. In my opinion, it was about 100 percent by the time it was over.

It was the most intense of all communities because up there on that mountain there were no men, and we were there making a revolution. There was *such* a feeling of empowerment. The teachers were empowering the students, and the students the teachers, and it was a wild thing. There were dances every night. I fell in love with another teacher—immediately. Now *this* was the really torrid affair. My twelve-year-old daughter was there. I didn't care if she knew. There were people of all ages. I was probably the oldest one. Well, not the oldest if you included all of the students (who were of all ages), but I turned forty-three that summer, which seemed mighty old. I had fantasies of leaving my husband and being with [this teacher], but when I got home, my old life resumed. It was going to be impossible, I felt. I couldn't do it.

Once I had fallen in love with women I knew that I was a person who falls in love with women; it was as simple as that. I no longer had any belief that women are divided up into homosexual or heterosexual or even bisexual. I do believe that everyone is everything and that circumstances have a lot to do with it. Of course, who you fall in love with is also a big mystery.

If there hadn't been a women's movement, I can imagine very easily that I might have spent the rest of my life

being resentful, rebellious, and bitchy—but on a personal basis, without having any way of actually coming
into my own. That's how it was in my first two marriages:
I *burned*, I *seethed*. But there was no way of doing anything
about it or describing it until the women's movement
gave me an explanation and something to be done. The
women's communities that I have been a part of have
stimulated and satisfied me immensely. Elsewhere I've
never found that kind of ecstatic feeling that I found in
the women's movement during those early years. After
the children had grown up, if there had still been the
kind of intense women's movement that was there when
my children were young, I might very well have given
up men.

I didn't feel qualms about manipulating men—I'm saying all of these terrible things—but would have felt bad
about manipulating women. I had to be honest with
women. It was part of my ideology and the ideology of
the women's movement. What would have been the
point to be dishonest with a woman, to act how I had
learned early to act with men? It was scary. I was very
comfortable being in charge, having the power in the relationship, which was what I could always have with
men. And being able to use the wiles I learned as a
child—there was pleasure in that comfort, familiarity. I
could count on it. But with women, it was so dangerous.
I didn't know what to expect. I couldn't rely on my manipulative powers.

With my last lover, the most intense one, I felt I didn't
have a right to be with her secretly once I realized that
I wasn't actually going to make the break from my
husband. It was hard. I didn't want to be one of those
women who was married but snuck around with women.
People resented that. No one ever said that they resented
it in me, although I'm sure my girlfriends' friends did. My

girlfriend wanted us to continue despite my husband and my need for secrecy, but I couldn't.

Despite how guilty, I felt [hurting this last girlfriend], falling in love with women was a great eye-opener for me. It enlarged my sense of myself. It made me . . . it was almost utopian in that it freed me from the given gender roles, what I had been devoting my life to doing. Now I understand that in some same-sex relationships people adopt gender roles anyway, but in my relationships we never did. It was illuminating. It was a physical demonstration that nothing is given. It really immensely fed my consciousness, and for that I will be forever grateful.

As Shulman's story indicates, there was a tremendous sense of utopia surrounding women's romantic love in the early second wave. There was also a belief that the behaviors women had learned as good little girls of the 1950s—being kittenish and passive, sating oneself with reflected glory—could be shed like a snake's skin with the addition of new, same-sex partners. Not only would evidence of women's oppressed, house-slave status, such as feminine wiles, be obliterated, but so would more mundane inequities, such as gender-mandated chore division. *Who is expected to do the dishes when you are both the same sex? Who fixes the car or picks up the groceries?* Finally, a kind of idealism was lodged in the belief that women's bodies were very different from men's yet perfectly able to satisfy other women, perhaps better than intercourse with men did. Twenty years earlier Kinsey's research revealed that lesbians had more orgasms than did heterosexual women. Certainly one wouldn't have to educate a feminist woman about that newly discovered jewel, the clitoris—they already knew! (Anne Koedt's 1970 article "The Myth of the Vaginal Orgasm" was enjoying great popularity—and it implicitly challenged men as ideal lovers from a sexual standpoint.) Men, for their part, were slow in adopt-

ing techniques to satisfy women. Indeed, one of the differences that most startled Kinsey in his 1950s studies of sexual behavior in women and men was that men would *never*
have put up with years of sex that didn't lead to orgasm.
Women routinely did. This begs two questions: Why were
women so self-negating, and why were men so inept?

Of course, some feminists had no compunction about
framing the problem and the solution very simply. "To give
a man support and love before giving it to a sister is to support [patriarchal] culture, that power system," wrote Rita
Mae Brown, the novelist and fearless activist for feminism
and gay rights. In second-wave histories, Brown comes off
as a swaggering figure, the Warren Beatty of the women's
liberation movement—beautiful, confident, and seductive.
Dramatic, if a bit too addicted to controversy, she was behind the lesbian takeover at the Second Congress to Unite
Women, in which the lights were extinguished and then
turned back on to reveal women decked out in LAVENDER MEN-
ACE T-shirts. That was a successful protest, among many, but
in the mid-seventies Brown's tenure with the Furies—a radical D.C. separatist group—is described in more harrowing
and even delusional terms. Furies members were asked
(some say ordered) to give up not just adult men but relationships with their own sons. Brown, famed for her verve
as well as for her first book, *Rubyfruit Jungle*, was then a
lothario, a sexually confident woman on the make. Separatist or not, the seduction style of Rita Mae Brown actually
makes the case that women can be just as aggressive as men.

Falling for other women—and swearing off men, whether
one's libido wanted to or not—served other profound, if
short-term, purposes, such as downplaying female competition. Personal ambition had become a deeply feared trait
among the seventies feminists; any vestige of it seemed
likely to puncture the fragile bubble of sisterhood they were
creating. Sisterhood was translated as "no one outshines

anyone else"—an ironic development, since the movement also promised women the liberation to be full human beings (which is a difficult achievement when you're being asked to hold back). A historian of the second wave, Sara Evans, refers to this type of conflict as "the threatened loss of new possibility," and asserts that feminist consciousness was born in that divergence.

Despite its being at the root of feminist uprising, female ambition, whether professional or sexual, was too often self-suppressed by these early radicals, as it had been suppressed earlier by a patriarchal culture. In memoirlike essays such as "On Trashing," by Jo Freeman, "Days of Celebration and Resistance," by Naomi Weisstein, and "To Hell and Back: On the Road with Black Feminism in the 1960s and 1970s," by Michele Wallace, movement sisters describe the pressure (both self- and movement-imposed) to temper their desires and talents. Old habits died hard: the feminist credo to value all women meant that women as individuals still played second fiddle—this time to a movement rather than to a man.

With respect to love, having romantic and sexual relationships with other women meant that those feminists had made an end-run around the nasty business of competing for (and desiring) male attention. It resolved a painful, if unacknowledged, tension: whichever friend a guy chooses, there's always the girl sitting there he didn't choose. Moreover, if being "chosen"—going after and receiving male attention—contributes to one's role as a sex object and not a full human being, then the "conscious" feminist can't comfortably engage in that behavior. However, if two women friends out at a bar have decided that they are going home together, they can neither be divided by a guy nor passively participate in the winner-loser game whereby only one is selected, and the other rejected. At least in the short term, they can have a love life *and* privilege women over men.

The stakes in making that choice were still high, as Kate Millett's treatment by *Time* signals. But the transformative power of aligning with other women was itself at an all-time high. Gloria Steinem held Millett's hand for an entire press conference after she was "outed," not because they were sleeping together, but because popular and demonstrably hetero Gloria wanted to convey that they were allies. The fact that so many second-wave women did indeed look both ways was overshadowed by an inability to see anything other than either homo- or heterosexuality. Since there wasn't a critical mass of women with consciousness about the value of their love for both men and women, many bisexual women didn't bother to try to describe themselves more clearly, finding that glossing it over as lesbian or straight was close enough.

Suppressing one's desires for men, even from within a lesbian relationship, isn't oppressive to all women who feel this sexual ambiguity. Dolores Alexander, a second-waver who came to feminism as a founder of NOW, told me that her basic sexuality is "probably heterosexual" but that "I felt that I could trust women so much more than I ever could trust a man."

Dolores was raised in an Italian Catholic family where men had all of the privilege and authority. She married relatively young, discovered feminism, and came out (or in) to the movement. Although she has thought about having a relationship with a man—"I've met guys I thought were attractive"—she knew "instinctively that I could never have the kind of relationship that I have with women with a man—the intimacy, the autonomy. It's just so much better and I can't duplicate it with a man. I would revert to old patterns and so would they—so, no, thanks. I would be trying to relate to a man because of social pressure, but I couldn't maintain my integrity within that relationship, I just know it." For Dolores, her real sexual preference might be characterized as straight, but not stupid—her orientation is toward a good relationship, and nothing is lost in her identifying simply as lesbian, despite her past and current desires.

Another prominent second-wave woman, the artist Linda Stein, told me:

> Speaking as a "mo" [homosexual], after spending my twenties and thirties trying to be a "tro" [heterosexual], I made a decision which I believe was more political than sexual. As a "tro" I was trained to defer to men, to hide my capabilities, to limit my potential. I wrote a piece (not submitted for publication) describing how I purposely threw the bowling ball into the alley, the Ping-Pong ball into the net, etc., so that the boy could be "better." I sat across from my date with an adoring look saying something like "Wow, you're a plumber. Tell me about it!" For me, life is better as a "mo."

In her 1973 book *Androgyny*, the late influential feminist professor Carolyn Heilbrun wrote, "I have learned that more people than we once thought are bisexual, and we are going to have to learn to be comfortable with that idea in the future." Heilbrun's glancing reference to the sexual choices that were irrevocably altering women's lives is a model of subtlety, pointing to a tiny shard of ice when in fact there was a huge iceberg.

As for me, I've been positively and heroically influenced by the pioneers of the second wave. Still, learning their stories makes me wonder why being attracted to men had to be invisible—even derided—by the same women who were fighting hard to live honest, full lives. Why was it so hard to acknowledge their many attractions? Was it that being involved with a man one desired might sabotage the subjectivity women experienced while creating a movement to liberate themselves? Did she fear that she couldn't be that independent "I am strong / I am invincible" roaring woman with a guy?

Meanwhile, the "political lesbian" idea that lesbians were morally superior—or even the natural authenticity of loving women—itself was a reflection of how dangerous it was to assert lesbian identity as anything other than perverse and pathological. This need to overstate the grandness of the Sapphic endeavor exposed not just the exuberance of a new convert, but a deep insecurity about being gay. Out and proud lesbianism was also so new, in terms of a public identity, that acknowledging the variety or ambiguities of the lesbian life—or the woman's life—was all but impossible. In the seventies, loving women almost had to take on a heroic cast—one that precluded looking back the other way again. This makes sense for the times. Many lesbians left gay rights movements (even as late as the 1980s with ACT UP) because women weren't a priority.

But below that egalitarian surface, there were psychological reasons to trumpet the virtues of being with women. When you are going against *everything* you have ever been raised to think about relationships, it helps to think of your "alternative choice" in messianic terms: men are part of the *patriarchy*, thus being with this woman creates an equal nonoppressive relationship. This is partly true, and feeling equal as a woman with a newly raised consciousness is a seductive thing, but this ideology keeps the sex and desire part of love secondary, taking it a step away from being "gay" (deviant!) and moving it into the realm of virtue. In some sense, having to (or choosing to) depict a woman's love life in such black-and-white, high-minded terms is less than liberated. Not only did it suppress the messier reality of many women's actual lives and desires, but it also reinforced a factional, and false, gay-straight split.

Radical second-wave women needed to experience something beyond the first flush of same-sex love even to excavate its complexity and problems. Being able to acknowledge problems in same-sex relationships, as we have learned to do in heterosexual ones, is a sign of strength in both the feminist and the gay rights movements. Inherent in our right to simply *be* is the right to be human. Or, as daughter of the second wave Ani DiFranco would later sing, we have the right to "do it all imperfectly."

CHAPTER 4

BISEXUALITY NOW: THE ANI PHENOMENON

If Anne Heche can play a lesbian, then God knows I can.

—Former *Dynasty* diva Joan Collins, making her case for a gay role at the 2001 GLAAD Media Awards

The very first article I ever wrote for publication was on the performance artist Diamanda Galas. I was twenty-three. I showed up for the interview at an East Village Polish restaurant without a tape recorder or notebook, informed Galas that I already knew what I wanted to write, and then chatted for about an hour as if out for tea with a friend. I was fortunate that she saw this as charming rather than infuriating. She hugged me at the end of our meeting as if to say, "You're pathetic, but young. You'll learn."

My second article was on a newish folk-punk singer named Ani DiFranco, who'd just come out with her sixth album, *Out of Range*. By the DiFranco interview I had learned a couple of things: (1) bring a notebook or tape recorder; and (2) get quotes. We met at the now-defunct coffee shop on Avenue A called Limbo. She ordered a lemonade and we shared it, like two bobby-soxers on a date, which I thought very cool of her. (Another interpretation: I still hadn't learned the most basic fundamentals of journalism: (3) don't drink from the interview subject's glass, she was simply showing forbearance.) Galas, who had performed at my

Wisconsin college naked except for fake blood and combat boots, had been two decades older than I and intimidating. DiFranco and I were the exact same age. She struck me as a great combination of Muppet-like goofiness and Ralph Nader–like intellectual seriousness. I loved her.

The article, which ran in *Ms.* in 1993, was DiFranco's first piece of national magazine press, and I continued to interview her over the years, for *Ms.*, *Glamour*, and *Playboy*, and to attend her shows. When Anastasia and I broke up, I listened to *Dilate* with unhealthy intensity, overrelating to DiFranco's songs of heartbreak. (Knowing that she ended up with the guy who was dragging her heart around in those songs made me sadder). One time, when Steven and I were in the process of making up, I saw Ani in an East Village bar with her ex-girlfriend and new boyfriend and it made me feel like she was some personal totem for me, blessing the Anastasia breakup while watching over my increasingly baroque love life. Of course she wasn't, really. She didn't know or care who I dated. But she had become a symbol for me, and a beacon for bisexual women.

In fact, no one has the ability to sum up feminist bisexuality the way Ani DiFranco does, both as an artist and in her private life. At her concerts the audience always moved me. The legions of women clad in hippie guerilla couture: combat boots, tattoos, crazy hair, and strappy tank tops with bras showing. The punk uniform signified a particular kind of third-wave rebellion to me. It was a marriage of feminine—the tight tops and the bra straps marking a contrast with the bralessness of second-wavers—with butch and tough (tattoos and combat boots, and sometimes shaved heads). The combination seemed to say that you could be both: you could be a girlie-girl and tough; you could be hot for women and men. Debbie Grossman, a New York photographer and photo editor, donned the Ani

DiFranco look when she moved to Manhattan to go to Barnard in 1995.

> I had black combat boots with rainbow laces and a pink triangle painted under the heel and like, these toilet cubes—those pull chains with the little beads? You get them at hardware stores—around my neck, lots of earrings. And then I got my nose pierced just like Ani, but on the *other* side so it wouldn't be exactly like her. People used to mistake me for her. One time, I bought a magazine with Ani on the cover, and some woman was like "Oh, is that you?" and that was so exciting. And to this day, teenage lesbians still look like that. I wonder where that style came from. It's like a little bit punk and a little hippie and . . . leather.

Beyond the aesthetic, at an Ani concert, girls you would otherwise think of as "just friends" become girlfriends. These young women hear Ani saying not simply that it's okay to be gay or bisexual, but also that a *girl is good*—to *be* and to sleep with. In idolizing Ani, they discover that crazy, hysterical passion that groupies and fans have long felt for their rock stars. For them, Ani is tapping into a history, an automatic attraction to rock stars as well as the androgyny and ambiguous sexual space that some popular musicians have always enjoyed (think Bowie, Michael Jackson—even Dolly Parton dresses like a drag queen). But loving Ani (or Amy Ray or The Butchies or Le Tigre) doesn't cut off the possibility of *being* her. This is crucial, since so much of women's desire for men can also be a desire to have what they have (success, ambition, freedom), as I felt so strongly with my depressed-but-successful writer beau, Steven. Ani DiFranco connects girls to a strong sense of their own sexuality, too. She models being unafraid of biting from the apple—it's fine to be sexual and experiment and to entertain all ideas. Through her music and her persona, she grants a lot of women access to that philosophy—and through her success and autonomy she raises the possibility of independence for her fans. "Ani was from the next town over," Debbie Grossman, who was raised in Rochester, New York, told me.

> My friends and I were obsessed with her records. It was like, "We're tough, we're gonna roam the streets at night and have adventures, and be alone in the world." We all went to a concert, and she was so hot, she still had the bald head at the time, and all the girls were like, "We're straight, but Ani is hot." She opened up feelings of wanting . . . it was just so different than any other kind of music or any other kind of woman. I mean, we all listened to other women who sang and wrote their own songs but we just all LOVED Ani, and loved every song.

The third wave, a beneficiary of the theories of the second wave, began thinking about love, sex, and identity at the place the second wave fought hard to get to: women were strong, could be independent, could have sex. Alix Kates Shulman's dilemma—pressure to call herself straight because it's not fair to fool around with women and also garner heterosexual privilege—had faded. So, too, had Dolores Alexander's problem—to be a lesbian, despite one's level of attraction to men, because one can't be both self-respecting and have a relationship with a guy. In fact, political pressure against bisexuality has abated somewhat, especially on college campuses. Women who look both ways might be part of hetero-feminist women's centers or they might organize with the queer kids—or they might be part of no particular group. The point is that they are here in record numbers. Today the gay rights movement often produces the most vibrant activism on college campuses. At the University of

Delaware, for instance, SAGE, the feminist group, has been on campus for a dozen years and has enjoyed a large annual budget due to fund-raising. Still, it is Haven, the university's newly formed gay rights group, that the progressive students support by attending their events in droves. "There is just a lot more excitement about Haven," says Constance DeCherney, the 2005 head of SAGE. "So we co-sponsor many of their events since they don't have a lot of money." That snapshot at University of Delaware is replicated across the country, especially at schools that have long had women's centers and courses in women's studies. As Felicia Kornbluh of Duke University put it, "My students have no idea what's going on with feminism, but they are all familiar with gay rights."

Meanwhile, as a fellow at Dartmouth College a few years ago, I was struck by how much the world had changed for gay students in the last decade. Dartmouth is not known for being a bastion of progressiveness, even among the Ivies. Bearing this out, the students I met during the fellowship categorically portrayed the social scene as dominated by frats. Excessive drinking was the main social activity, and I was surprised by the number of nineteen-year-olds who claimed to have their hearts already set on investment banking jobs, skipping over the idealistic Peace Corps stint altogether. As conservative as Dartmouth is in some respects, when it comes to campus queer activities, it has reflected the national mood of rapid change. By spring of 2004, when I visited the campus, it had five GLBT groups, four queer studies courses, a coordinator of GLBT programming and advocacy, a GLBT resource room, and a network for out and allied students called Queer Peers.

The class of 2004 was remarkable for being "out" from the moment they hit campus. Other alums traveled back to Dartmouth for that year's celebration, and each noted how much courage and self-respect they garnered from these younger students' confident, actualized attitudes. One man who had himself suffered through being queer at Dartmouth while a student there in the early 1980s started to cry when he recalled that he had been deeply closeted as an undergraduate—and the one student he knew of who was openly gay was so ostracized that he had to leave school. So much had changed in two decades.

The gay rights and women's movements have progressed exponentially from their late-sixties and second-wave incarnations. And whether or not younger women (and men) call themselves feminists, their lives have been profoundly changed by the philosophy and activism of the women's liberation movement. Who these women were and how they agitated from the halls of Congress to the cul de sacs of suburbia to alter society isn't as well known as it should be. But the result of their efforts is that people my age and younger knew girls who were incredibly strong and talented athletes; we witnessed that girls could wrestle in junior high (and, more recently, in the Olympics), and play professional basketball. Some of our peers enrolled in advanced math and science classes, and women could go to any college and aspire to any profession. *Date rape, battered women's syndrome, sexism*—all were terms coined at least a generation ago, and all enabled women of the third wave to describe injustice, discover those affected, and seek resources designed to combat these oppressions once just called life.

Similarly, gay rights—and gay people—are integrated into our world in a way that would have been unimaginable thirty years ago. Lesbians are out in high school and, in some cases, getting lucky—thus providing an interesting alternative to the studly senior guy. An ethic of equality (if not quite the reality of equality) is integrated into American culture today. The women's movement may no longer be the brash, new, highly visible, media-attractive entity it was when first organizing itself, but its reach and its root system are far greater. Meanwhile, gay rights is the media-attractive entity feminism once was. Even if the story is bad news about anti–gay marriage referendums or the fact that a school board would rather get rid of all clubs than allow a gay-straight alliance, it's much more likely for a queer story to lead the news today than it is for a feminist story to do so. And bisexuality is a big, though submerged, part of that phenomenon.

The exact date that bisexuality became common for younger women is hard to determine. In my view, it coincides roughly with the last days of the first Bush administration and Ani DiFranco's rapid permeation of collegiate record collections. "I remember when it changed on campuses, at least from my perspective," Gloria Steinem, the feminist writer and second-wave icon, told me. "It was 1990. Suddenly, it was okay to be bisexual." Indeed, that was when college gay rights groups were active even at my very straight (or so I assumed) Midwestern school, Lawrence University, in Appleton, Wisconsin. Our gay rights organization fattened its roster with several self-identified bisexual women. Major gay lobbying organizations, such as the Human Rights Campaign, had adopted bisexuality as part of their mission a bit earlier—in HRC's case, by 1983—and organizations founded later, such as the Gay Lesbian Straight Education Network (GLSEN), founded in 1995, always had bisexuality as a part of their mandate. Still, it wasn't until 1993 that the March on Washington for gay rights explicitly included bisexuals, despite the fact that they'd been marching as an identified group periodically since 1979. That inclusive 1993 march followed the founding of a vibrant younger lesbian-feminist activist group, the Lesbian Avengers, initiated in 1992 by writer Sarah Schulman and other women active in New York's ACT UP. In other words, the daughters of feminism felt freer to include in the queer conversation their bisexuality, which had existed (at least in subtext or controversy) for every generation.

The impact of third-wave queers on the visibility of bisexuality was considerable. Beginning in the nineties, gay visibility in general became commonplace. The comic lesbian love story *Go Fish* was the surprise toast of Sundance in 1993. In 1995, gossip columns reported that Jane Pratt, editor of the much-beloved *Sassy* and soon-to-be-editor of *Jane*, was rolling around at parties with Drew Barrymore (*and* Michael Stipe—who turned out to be bisexual as well). At that time, I wrote the "feminist gossip column" at *Ms.* magazine; it was short-lived, since *Ms.*'s earnest readership and feminist ethics didn't facilitate my hunting down lurid stories. I called Pratt for comment. She was clearly taken aback, especially since the call was from anti-celebrity, ad-free *Ms.*, but she replied, "While I don't want to condone gossip, if my appearance in the media linked with Drew makes someone else feel good about their choice, then that's fine with me. *Utterly.*" She added: "It's no more odd to be linked with Drew than it would be with Tom Cruise." (Of course, a decade later one might say that nothing is more odd than being linked with Tom Cruise.) Something had changed. By contrast, my call to then editor of *Cosmo* Helen Gurley Brown, another much-loved and influential girlie feminist editor, but from another generation, yielded different results. I asked her if *Cosmopolitan* would ever include a bisexual audience. "No," the original girlie answered without hesitation. "*Cosmo* is for women who love men." (I did end up getting some good historical gossip from Brown, though. One niblet: When *Ms.* was first launched, Gloria Steinem reached out to Brown to present the new, inexperienced staff with the secrets of successful magazine publishing. HGB did, and received a Tiffany key chain inscribed MS., which she carried for years.)

Still, Brown was a very sophisticated Los Angeles chick, hardly in denial about the existence of gay people. In her forward-thinking yet man-catching guide, *Sex and the Single Girl* (the publishing sensation of 1962), she writes the following under the heading "Suppose You Like Girls":

> You've already worked out a way of life for yourself to which I could contribute no helpful advice. I'm sure your problems are many. I don't know about your pleasures. At any rate, it's your business and I think it's a shame you have to be so surreptitious about your choice of a way of life.

Brown predated the second wave—*Sex and the Single Girl* came out a year ahead of *The Feminine Mystique*—but the idea that someone who wanted to be a *Cosmo* girl might also *fancy* a *Cosmo* girl was way off her radar. Reading the Brown quote now, I'm both impressed that she mentioned same-sex attraction at all and shocked that she dispensed with it in a curt four sentences. Whereas, Drew Barrymore, a daughter of the second wave, doesn't even bat an eye at the thought—she completely embraces it. As late as 2003 she said, "Do I like women sexually? Yeah, I do. Totally." In the intervening years, girlie-girls were known to date girls. The old image of a queer(ish) woman (picture Candace Gingrich or Martina Navratilova) had broadened—it could be any woman.

"Sexuality cannot be abstracted from its surrounding social layers," write Ellen Ross and Rayna Rapp, historians and anthropologists, in the anthology *Powers of Desire: The Politics of Sexuality*. Indeed, the several decades of feminism had changed society, and the younger feminists were building on the insights of their mothers, stretching the boundaries within which seventies feminists had worked. In the seventies, there was a way to *look* like a feminist. You didn't look masculine, like those unevolved bar dykes. You didn't wear high heels and hairdos like unevolved hausfraus. You were *natural*—although natural meant no makeup and frequently ethnic clothing that bore no relationship to your own ethnicity. The girls growing up in that half-finished revolution started from a different place than their mothers and foremothers. Purely as a consequence of evolution, they were more likely to openly look both ways. They also reacted to the perceived sense that a lesbian or a feminist must appear a certain way, and therefore dressed to interrupt the assumptions of what a feminist looks like.

I met Liza Featherstone at *Ms.* magazine when I was twenty-two and she was twenty-three. She was the adorable, tall, hairy-legged freelance fact-checker who came in during closing (the end of production for an issue). Today she is a writer and contributing editor for *The Nation*. Then she had girlfriends, today she is married to a man. Liza's experience as a bisexual woman subverted outdated expectations of femininity for straight and gay women:

> It was funny because dressing girlie felt more lesbian to me, but it looked straighter in a larger sense of the world. I used to wear my boyfriend's clothes if I really liked them, but with my girlfriend it just seemed so important that we were stylistically different. With men I would often go around looking schlumpy. With her, I didn't. It was partly because I wanted to make sure I looked good as the trophy girlfriend, but it was also that we were on display. People are looking at you, you gotta look good. I mean everyone is going to look at you if you're two lesbians, even in Manhattan. You feel much more like you have to be ready to greet the public. It really is much more like being a famous person. I'm sure there's a lot of privilege in experiencing it that way, living in New York and all kinds of things. But to see it as a performance

rather than as something scary is a nice historical position to be in.

Women today are raised in an environment rich with queer pop culture. Back when I was a Cap'n Crunch–smacking kid glued to the tube, Jack Tripper had to pretend he was fruity on *Three's Company* so that his stodgy, sex-averse landlord, Mr. Roper (and later Mr. Furley, who was presumed to be straight, but wore a lavender ascot), would allow him to share an apartment with two chicks in tight slacks who happened to share a bedroom. Jack's ability to swish whenever Mr. Roper got suspicious gave the show its raison d'être and a significant portion of its laugh lines. Interest in gay people on TV other than as obvious "light in his loafers" jokes was nearly nonexistent at the time. I had no idea that the Village People were representing gay iconography when I saw them on *American Bandstand* in 1979. I just thought they had cool costumes: you know, a cop, a construction worker, a leather daddy . . . Thanks to Madonna, a direct conduit between gay urban club culture and suburban mall rats, I knew what was up by the late eighties. Still, despite Madonna, queer representation in popular culture was either coded (some people "got it," most did not) or homophobic (Jack Tripper et al.), until the AIDS crisis.

Much as identifying men as the patriarchy incarnate gave women the strength—and a political reason—to look both ways and take a woman as a partner, the AIDS crisis made coming out of the closet a deeply moral stance. Egged on by gay journalists and activists, some stars took up the call, risking losses in record sales and corporate sponsorship. The Indigo Girls came out publicly in *Out* magazine in 1989, the same year as their platinum debut album. Then came Melissa Etheridge in 1993, largely in response to falling in love with Julie Cypher. Cypher left her husband,

actor Lou Diamond Phillips, for Etheridge and went on to
have two well-publicized procreative moments with her before they split up in 2000. In 1992, Canadian crooner k. d.
lang let it be known that she was gay. The musician Meshell
Ndegeocello was open about her bisexuality when her debut album, *Plantation Lullabies*, was making a stir in 1993.
Friends had a two-moms storyline that began with their
initial episode and carried on throughout the first season,
culminating in a gay wedding. Soon almost every major,
slightly edgy TV show had a gay or bisexual character, from
Will and Grace to *ER* to *Roseanne*. Pop culture wasn't the only
reflection of the rapid rise of the gay rights movement in
the eighties and nineties. It was seen also in generational
differences within families. My friend Pete's older (by decades) sister Joan finally came out in the 1980s, after years of
referring to her girlfriend as her "roommate." At the same
time Joan was in the closet, Pete, who is straight, was a
member of ACT UP.

The most highly awaited and sensational coming-out
ever was that of Ellen DeGeneres, the star of the hit show
Ellen. Her unveiling was hinted at for months before the
episode and her announcement spawned a flurry of magazine stories, including the "Yep, I'm Gay" *Time* magazine
cover. Ellen's coming-out would have been huge regardless,
given that her show was number thirteen in the Nielsens
at the time and enjoyed a weekly viewership of forty-two
million. Still, what truly made Ellen's outing Princess
Di–level scintillating was her new girlfriend, Anne Heche.
Anne was a well-regarded if little-known denizen of indie
films such as *Walking and Talking* and a veteran of the soap
opera *Another World*, on which she played, quite expertly, the
twins Marley (who was good and dull and wore mauve) and
Vicky (who was bad and ballsy and wore black). One week
after they 'started dating, Ellen's character came out on air.

Amid dozens of media moments, she and Heche appeared on *Oprah* together holding hands, not as "sisters" like Kate Millett and Gloria Steinem, but as "wives."

Pop culture is derided for mining political movements and selling them back to us neutered of politics—a Black Panther beret or a Girl Power T-shirt—but at the same time the positive force of pop culture is misunderstood. The *Ellen* show and Ellen DeGeneres's personal coming-out significantly eased my transition from solely straight to bisexual. Through Ellen, my mother could look beyond Elton John— so unstable!—to this attractive, subtle, funny, blond lady whose work she loved. It was less of a leap from Ellen to me than from Elton to me, and that was reassuring for one and all. I didn't have to spend so much time explaining everything to my mother because gay people were already part of her cultural conversation. More than that, the coming-out of someone cool and successful like Ellen conveyed the okayness of being gay. *Having a girlfriend doesn't have to condemn you to a life of shadowy despair.*

My generation's overt use of pop culture to spread politics is unique. You see it with feminism (à la Riot Grrls) and civil rights (à la hip-hop). Every other generation used it covertly, of course, from Shakespeare's sonnets to his male friend to Marlene Dietrich's tux and top hat in *Morocco*. This "delicious subtext" can be seen in Doris Day's portrayal of *Calamity Jane*, or via unsavory literature, such as pulp novels, and is, I suppose, indicative of an unfinished revolution. Just because we can identify exploitation and even laugh at it doesn't mean that we are no longer exploited. Similarly, just because there are gay characters on every sitcom doesn't mean one can get partner health benefits. Furthermore, for everyone like Ellen, who is "out" and basically okay, there is someone like Jodie Foster, who isn't out, or someone like Rosie O'Donnell, who came out and whose appeal coincidentally plummeted. As much progress as there was, women still experienced much that is damaging.

Many people think of Anne Heche as the Bad Bisexual, the one who left America's lesbian sweetheart, having destroyed (at least temporarily) Ellen's career by encouraging her to be so public and out and *gay!* ("Anne just didn't have the instincts of a gay person," a lesbian professor at Oregon State University told me. It was the most succinct assessment among the many I have heard.) Ellen finished up 2000 shell-shocked and sitcom-less, while Anne married, had a baby, and wrote a book all in the same year. But just as there is a good witch to counteract the bad, there is a Good Bisexual icon, and she is, of course, Ani DiFranco.

The first time I saw her perform, at a folk festival in New Jersey, I was shocked by her lyrics—she sang as if she felt exactly the way I felt: furious about street harassment, titillated by sexual attention, energized by feminism, daunted by all the injustice in the world, and intermittently positive that she could kick anyone's ass. Ani is that daughter of the second wave, somewhat bruised and exploited as she felt her way through early heterosexual relationships, drawn to power, and also drawn to empowerment. To wit, when my former intern Liz Maki was sixteen, in 2000, she spent the summer at a young writer's workshop at Simon's Rock, in Barrington, Massachusetts. Ani was the place's lingua franca. Liz recalls:

> There were eighty girls but only sixteen boys at Simon's Rock. Partly because of the lack of eligible boys, and partly because a lot of the kids were gay and out, and partly because it fit in with their ideas of being writers— beatnik, sexually ambiguous—everyone said that they were bi. That was the first place that I have ever been where the whole community was solidly obsessed with Ani DiFranco. I think it is because she says it's okay to be

queer. As soon as I got to camp, it was like, "Do you like Ani DiFranco?" "How many times have you seen her?" She was the household word. It was kind of a shock to me because I didn't know that that many people knew about her or listened to her.

As for the boys at Simon's Rock, there wasn't that "Can I watch?" vibe. A lot of the guys were openly bi themselves, first of all, but they weren't jocks who needed to protect their position—they were the kind of guys who go to writing camp. Plus, there were more than enough girls to go around for the guys who were interested.

It was the weirdest example of adolescent sexuality I had ever seen. There was this girl who was the ringleader—she hooked up with many people. The very first night she introduced herself and said she was "looking for a partner." Many of her hookups were *not* girls you would think of as being into experimenting, but this girl could seduce them. Her e-mail address was Anifan. She goes to Smith now.

According to Liz, a lot of the Ani talk was just saying which songs you liked—"I like 'Two Little Girls' a lot," she offers—but that was really about communicating through the messages Ani was conveying. "She's an underdog and rebellious and independent—kids like that," Liz says. The love object in many of Ani's songs is sexually ambiguous, which appeals to teenagers and young people. "It's another space outside of a label or a group," Liz says. Music is a way of connecting to something bigger. As she puts it: "One of the first questions you get asked as a teenager is 'What kind of music do you listen to?' and the answer tells you a lot about whether you'll like the person."

Angela Maria DiFranco was born in Buffalo, New York, on September 23, 1970, the second child of Elizabeth and

Dante DiFranco. Her dad was passive and distracted, and Ani (her nickname from childhood) identified strongly with her mom, a stubborn independent redhead who went to MIT in the 1950s, rode a motorcycle, and went by the nickname Pete. Ani's older brother was rebellious and took up a majority of her parents' time, so the future feminist folkie was left to her own devices early in her life, which she really didn't mind. Initially, her mother was strict, but when the precocious Ani was at a young age her mother said, "You're a person, I respect you," and became an utterly supportive, extremely confident "I-trust-your-judgment" and "you-can-be-whatever-you-want" mom. At age fifteen, DiFranco decided to move to New York City. Her parents had split up four years earlier, and Ani had already begun hanging out in bars in Buffalo, playing music and having affairs with much older men in the scene.

Me and my best girlfriend from the preteen and under days, we used to get married all of the time. I was kind of a tomboy so I'm thinking that I was the groom mostly, but we switched off. When I started actually dating people, though, I was a teenage girl with older men. It's a common syndrome for teenage girls to learn sex with a much older guy, but in my case, I had a lot of opportunity. I was working, living on my own, and playing out in bars. I was kind of passing in the adult world a lot. I was with my first lover for three and a half years and I never *came*. It wasn't until I was probably eighteen or nineteen that, you know, that happened for the first time. Now I'm in my thirties and quite honestly, I feel like I am only beginning to awaken to my sexuality. I am totally beginning to *see* people—really see people—I don't even know what the word is, but see their *chi*, or their force, what is powering them around the earth. And they are of different natures—and some strike me as very feminine, some masculine. I had a lover once who was this beautiful woman, and she was like a goddess, she just seemed to embody femininity—*so gorgeous*. And there are creatures out there that just seem so masculine and they just embody masculine energy . . . and they're not always guys. And then there is all of this territory in between.

As for my story, my relationships with women weren't until I was in college. I showed up at the New School for Social Research and sat down in my first feminism class. There was this girl there—we just locked eyes and that was pretty much the first woman I ever fell in love with. I didn't think about gender, I thought, *here is a captivating person, meeting my energy and intensity and making me want to know more.*

This first girlfriend had kind of moved to New York to be a lesbian. She wanted to leave the claustrophobia of where she came from to shed her family. So she showed up in New York like, "I'm going to be a dyke now." I wasn't making a big statement about [the inadequacy of my earlier relationships] by being with her; I was just following my spleen. In general, I just follow my instincts. But I mean, [those old relationships] simply weren't working for me anymore. I find I don't have to calculate those sorts of shifts; I just listen. And when your body is involved, you know, it's pretty hard to ignore the calls of your body. Being with women was a really wonderful place to get to as a young woman. You are raised in this patriarchy where you are taught to be competitive with other young women and you finally get to the point where your own will just dictates that you stop that and you build community with them. So that was certainly a wonderful shift.

Loving women helps a young feminist change her role within patriarchy. The third-wave filmmaker Elisabeth Subrin asks in her short film *Swallow*, "if we were all liberated in the seventies, how come my generation was sticking their heads in the toilet in the eighties?" In fact, two issues that separate this generation of feminists from their mothers are the prevalence of eating disorders and bisexuality—and they are certainly linked. When women began trying to move around the world unshackled to what had been their identities (their relationship to men), they had to seek other ways to generate a sense of security and stability. In this society, control or power is a sign that you are an adult, a free agent, stable and replete with responsibilities. But over whom or what does a woman exercise control in a male-ruled society? Herself. The anorexic, the cutter, the girl who burns herself—all are playing out master and slave in a body that owns both, from a half-completed transformation initiated by feminism. When you hear a girl explaining why she starves herself, she invariably says that she felt addicted to the sense of power over herself, the control, and the thought of losing that control was terrifying.

Now, on a less damaging note, if you seek sexual power that is active, not simply seductive, over whom will you have it? A woman. With whom can you insert yourself into the male gaze of sexual advantage? Well, you can step into *his* birthright if you check out girls. In response to a question about extracurricular ogling by her boyfriend, one *Glamour* reader says that "Nine times out of 10, I check out girls more than my boyfriend does. Isn't that one way we women gauge our own looks?"[24]

Of course, there is something ridiculous about competing with men to check out women, as Ariel Levy argues in her 2005 polemic *Female Chauvinist Pigs*. Women check out women in part to compete with one another, which could be called a masculine motivation. But gazing along with the men also defeats sexism, because male supremacy is predicated on *exclusive* advantages based on sex; when we women join in, we drain that exclusive power. Checking out women is also simply fun and sexy, rather than a strategy to undermine patriarchy—and lesbians and bisexuals (and, increasingly, straight women) know all of this. Butch lesbians can take pride in being manly; lesbians with pretty trophy girlfriends can act as men do. Amy Ray used to cop to the fact that she could get the hot chicks and competed with men for them—and I was flattered, perhaps delusionally, to be her trophy girlfriend. In a new twist on Gloria Steinem's adage "we're becoming the men we wanted to marry," women no longer have to *become* sexy supermodels—they can simply date them, as Sandra Bernhard has done with Patricia Velasquez and as sexy British guitarist Alice Temple did with early-nineties glamazon Rachel Williams. And if *we* do it, is it still sexism? Not exactly. The Scores strip club may be seedy and disgusting, but it's the fact that women (other than those who dance there) can't come in unless they have a male escort that truly makes it sexist.

Ani experienced the joy of bonding with women after years of feeling not just competitive, but also that the company of girls was somehow retrograde. Soon she was spreading the "girl is good" word through her songs and persona. Her first record came out in 1990, but she was already a phenomenon on the northeastern college circuit. As happy and successful as she was, the triumphant spirit of her same-sex relationships brought some complications. "I found that when I began having women lovers it was much scarier . . . I was terrified. I was absolutely terrified by my women lovers in a way that men don't terrify me at all. I felt really seen and like I can't pretend."

Alix Kates Shulman also refers to the automatic lack of artifice in romantic relationships with women, which makes one wonder if men are similarly terrified of women lovers—pointing to some sort of penetrating emotional insight that only women possess—or if it is simply the likeness that makes women so sure their female lovers would be hip to any tricks. (In that case, perhaps men are more nervous around male lovers.) Either way, there is a pattern of women attempting to heal from patriarchy's wounds (female competition, fear and loathing of our bodies, doormat-itis) through intimacy with women and hiding emotionally with men. Both male and female lovers can be really hot, deeply loving, and important. It's just that the first underscores our damage as women; the other has more potential to enact new damage. As Ani puts it:

> There is an otherness in hetero relationships, if I can generalize about one aspect of it. There's that kind of mystery amongst genders and therefore, there are places to hide—for women, certainly. Not so much for men because—again, to generalize—women are a little bit more intuitive and often looking beneath the surface when a man will be looking at the surface. That exposure was scary to me. I think I was used to hiding, you know, with these old guys. In my mind I was free, but in my spirit . . . I mean I didn't think I was going to grow old and die with this person or that person and I was even trying to orchestrate the end for maybe longer than I should have with some of my early relationships. Still, the actual circumstance, I was playing along and being very happy and very nice. There was kind of the game of men and women that I learned to play very young, almost as a child. Sure, *that* you can always fall back on. We know it by the time we grow our first pubic hair. I think that my falling in love with another girl just inherently shed a lot of those games. There wasn't any place to hide.

Ani also rejected the notion of "coming out." While I don't exactly relate to that touchstone gay moment myself, I have to admit that I repeatedly go through my own special bisexual form of it, having to explain my life with each relationship I am in. Rather than being "closeted," I feel forced to be a host, guiding the uninitiated on through Sexuality 101. The constant negotiating one has to do in the face of fear of same-sex relationships is draining. I felt how tedious and painful it could be during the years I brought Amy Ray home with me for Christmas. I always felt as if I had to be doubly sure to be the "same old Jenny"—friendly, feminine, social—in order to cut off at the pass any stereotypes or social discomfort. I was aware that people might simply not know what to say when I introduced my girlfriend, not out of hatred but out of pure lack of experience. I was always conscious of trying to ease that transition for others, and it was, at times, oppressive, even though self-imposed. Ani, too, does not relate to the term *coming out*:

> I didn't "come out." There was never any in. To me, to come out is to reveal your great secret and I never had a secret. My way of coming out about everything is to write a song about it and I have always done that along the way. I must say that there was always a little awkward tension with my mother about [my girlfriends]. She would suspect that some of my female friends were [lovers] . . . and she'd try to be supportive and say, "Maybe you want to come visit with your friend, *what's-hername?*" But there was never really a verbalizing of any of it.

Ani has written eloquently about patriarchy and girl power. Her songs, which have become mantras for a generation of feminists, include "Not a Pretty Girl," in which she made *pretty* synonymous with compliant and weak. She growled, "I ain't no damsel in distress / and I don't need to be rescued / So put me down punk / Wouldn't you prefer a maiden fair / Isn't there a kitten caught up in a tree somewhere?" She wrote about her abortion ("Tiptoe"), sexual abuse ("Letter to a John"), and one-night stands ("Shy"). Moreover, she has remained independent and self-made in a business that has been historically hard on women. According to *Inc.* magazine, "her record company, Righteous Babe Records, is one of the few successful artist-created labels around, having sold more than 4 million of DiFranco's records and put out CDs by more than a dozen other performers. And it's no ordinary company . . . Staff members . . . respond with handwritten notes to the thousands of letters the company gets from its customers, DiFranco's fans."[25]

As DiFranco became more famous, and her life began to change, her girl-love/girl-power narrative began to shift:

> I came from a community of young women where we were all unguarded with each other and affectionate and absolutely enamored—it was school and New York and Feminism 101 and the theater group I was in and basically all of the women that I met at school. And then what happened is that I left that community and I got in a van with a guy—a very hetero guy—and I did that for six years. Then, there were two guys, and I did that for another few years, and now there are twelve guys. So the whole cultural landscape of my life changed. Not only that—worse than that—not only was my community of women gone, meaning all of my friends, but then young women just became . . . *fans*. That brought on this whole shift in my personality. I find myself attracted to strength—and fooled very often by what I perceive as strength. But when every young woman who comes up to talk to you, no matter how vibrant or dynamic they are, if they come up to you kind of *shaking* and kind of *panting*, it's just not sexy.
>
> But *men* still treated me . . . well, there was none of that

kind of adulation, which preserved attraction. The other funny thing about it is that the kind of songs that I write mean that females in my audience are usually more aggressive and demanding than the males. The guys that show up are the sensitive guys who are sitting there and trying to be cool enough to hang with feminists. Meanwhile the feminists are screaming at me about what I should be doing at every moment. I developed this very strange relationship with my own kind, which I have also just been getting over. You know, a few years have gone by and I'm a little less one of them. I'm not quite as young on the young woman continuum. I almost feel like I have more room for it now. More tolerance of needy or aggressive young women in my life—of which there are many.

A lot of airtime has been given to my struggle with my audience; it's almost been exaggerated to the point of it being distorted because the other side of it is that they've given me a job. While they were annoying the fuck out of me for years and becoming people I would escape from—I would duck down in the van and Andy [Stochansky, her drummer at the time] would screech away so that whatever psycho chick was stalking me at the time didn't see us. And yet, looking back, I'm just now beginning to see how much of myself those other young women gave me. For instance when I started playing music, my insecurities were just raging. I would bring the insecurities onstage, and I would make people uncomfortable. From years and years of interactions with people who are really nervous and fluttering, gasping and gulping—are playing very weak to my very strong—means that I became strong in a way that I never would have on my own. I never would have been as confident as I am now, just one on one. Because I never was that confident all-powerful Amazon that they were making me out to be, but when enough people are pretending you are that, it just becomes a part of your perception of yourself, at least in my case, enough to finally shed the self-consciousness. The constant self-hatred, the panic of standing onstage and the *I'm zitty and I'm pale and I'm fat and I can't believe I wore this thing that keeps coming open and I'm singing terribly tonight.* That used to be my whole experience of performing. I'd be the only person in the room not having fun.

So while these young women were driving me nuts, they were also showing me that there is nothing wrong with me. With vehemence they were saying you are so good, you are so strong, you are beautiful, you are my heroine. After a while, when you have a lot of interactions with people who are affirming you, it changes you. For a lot of performers or rock stars it can do things to you that are destructive or unfortunate but it's really been helpful to me.

It wasn't simply people's affirmation of her that enabled Ani to confront her insecurity. It was also that young women were loving her and she had loved women—she had found what it was to love in women, not just her observation of women's power to seduce powerful guys—she experienced what was truly valuable in people like her. This helped her to purge some of her own internalized misogyny. Then, in the mid-nineties, Ani fell in love with a man. In 1998, she married him. They've since split up, but she spoke of how marriage affected her: "Marrying a man was interesting. In retrospect, there was a lot of fabrication of turmoil between my audience and myself that I bought into; I can't think around my marriage actually of a single incident where someone in my audience said, 'You betrayed me,' to my face. I just read that everywhere." And the critique stung.

When last we spoke in the summer of 2006, she had just found out she was pregnant. While writing this book, I got pregnant with Gordon, my partner after Amy. When Amy and I broke up and with the ensuing male lover and then pregnancy, I suddenly appeared straight. I did not need to fret when Dad referred to Amy, my lover of five years, as "Jenny's friend" on the phone to Grandma Gladys. (Grandma Gladys knew Amy was my girlfriend, but I felt occasional awkwardness around that label with anyone over sixty-five, which was misplaced, considering that my Aunt Joyce referred to me as AC/DC to my face at my grand-mother's ninetieth birthday party.) But I also no longer had a special, automatic bond with the queer faculty at the schools I traveled to on book tours, many of whom had come out in middle age after years of being closeted and seemed, because of the risks they took in the face of dis-crimination, brave and serious. Their warmth toward me made me feel important and brave as well.

After Amy, I felt vulnerable in a new way when I was ad-dressing the college audiences that have become a part of my life since writing my first book. All of the baby dykes and gorgeous tomboys, the Women's Studies professors with brush cuts or purple T-shirts, the community I so ef-fortlessly connected with for the last five years—I feared that we wouldn't connect anymore. I wondered if Jennifer without a girlfriend was just a straight girl, but at the same time I didn't feel that straight girls were "just" straight girls. Still, this sense of being stripped of some laurel or a valu-able piece of one's identity is particular to bisexual women.

Who "makes" me feel that way, as if I'm fraudulent? As if I can no longer be part of this queer women's world I was so connected to? I fear it's simply me—due to an internalized inability to practice what I preach. But it's also a function of the fear and loathing of gay people that predicates the separation into straight and gay cultures. The gay side is morally superior—if you have ever witnessed the processing at a *Ms.* editorial meeting or the breakout session at the Michigan Womyn's Music Festival for chemical-free S/M Marxist feminists, you will know what I mean—but the straight side is more valued. In this worldview, the woman who looks both ways has potential (ineluctable) to be upwardly mobile (dating men) and also a betrayer of her ghettoized roots. Ani DiFranco experienced the tension between the two soon after her marriage.

I got a queer music award after I got hitched—it's called a GLAMA. Apparently, there was some controversy about whether I was queer enough to receive it. I heard about the debate over whether I should even be considered and I thought that sucked, that an organization that was there to affirm people's love was engaging in this. Especially since, well, quite honestly, the sexual relationship with the person that I married was the most queer sexual relationship I have ever had. He's technically a boy and I am technically a girl, but that was fluid for us. So it was like, here I found a boy with this equipment that I am so fond of and who is this completely open, making-it-up-as-we-go-along kind of genderless freak in bed. So for the "queer community" to say that this relationship disqualifies me is a fundamentally different idea of queerness than the one I have. Ironically, it was Sara Lee [the redheaded bass player who toured with Ani for many years in addition to playing with the B-52s and Indigo Girls] who gave me the award. Sara is bi as the day is long. Gay rights should never be about forcing people to be gay just because they believe in it. [In the GLAMA world of 2000], bisexuality doesn't seem like something that could really exist; I got married so I am straight, and Sara has a girlfriend so she is gay.

When I was twenty-two and barely out of college, *The Mists of Avalon* was published. It was a huge hit, especially in New Age feminist circles, and read by many of my most trusted female friends. But, just as with *The Red Tent* in the mid-nineties, I carried around the chunky paperback for months and couldn't get into it. There is one feature of the novel, though, that bears telling here as an analogy for the plight of the bisexual woman in a gay-straight world. Avalon is an island that you can go to only when you're ready, and it exists only if you can go to it. You travel to Avalon by boat, and the boat emerges out of the mist only if you are meant to be there. Unless you are ready, chosen, and want it, Avalon doesn't exist for you. Once you get there, it's perfect and magical, though a bit small. Avalon is wonderful, but if you leave, you leave—there is no regular ferry service between this beautiful utopia and the regular world you've known.

Anastasia was one of those friends who loved *The Mists of Avalon* and in fact told me about getting to Avalon. We discussed it one night after I began dating Gordon and she was with her fourth boyfriend after Marge, the woman for whom she'd broken up with me. Avalon was such an obvious metaphor for the lovely margins made by feminists and lesbians—the Michigan Womyn's Music Festivals and the Women's Studies programs—which, because they can't be integrated, are by definition something you have to leave in order to grow as a person. If I had only ever worked as an editor at *Ms.* magazine—the one magazine without ads—I would always wonder if I had what it took to make it at a mainstream publication, even if I was able to maintain my belief that *Ms.* was a morally superior job. Moreover, I believe that everyone on Avalon should be able to come and go. If Avalon is women-only life, then I want my relationship with lesbians—with all women—to be strong regardless of whom I date. And vice versa: I want to feel that my life with women doesn't preclude real connections with men.

"All I can say," Ani DiFranco told me as we concluded our interview,

> is thank god that scads of young people can just proclaim themselves bisexual now. Whatever that means to them, and wherever they are going to go from there, who cares? I'm just so gratified to see the world changing. Whether that happens at fifteen or at fifty, just imagining that you have the liberty—the choice—is the important thing.
>
> I had a really crazy, fucked-up family but my parents—bless their hearts—gave me this fearlessness. Like you asked me did I experience any tension or fear walking down the street with my girlfriend, and I was trying to imagine myself being afraid of fucking anybody telling me that I can't become myself.

CHAPTER 5

GAY EXPECTATIONS

If I'm going to be a wife, I damn well get to have one, too.

—Jan Clausen, from her 1999 memoir *Apples and Oranges*

I have been engaged in my ideal relationship for years. I have a partner, in fact, who shares not only tedious tasks with me, such as standing in line at the post office or cleaning behind the couch, but also fun things. This partner has traveled with me around the country, from scary Motel 6 stays in central Pennsylvania to spa days in Hawaii. We have supported each other through good and bad; we laugh constantly, cry occasionally, rarely fight, and have met (and get along with) our entire extended and chosen families. The only rub is that this ideal coupling is actually with my writing partner, Amy Richards. I've thought about my relationship with Amy often over the last few years, because it is my most successful and egalitarian relationship. We're not in love, but it would be great to be in love and be in the kind of relationship we have. I think it's what I keep assuming I'll find eventually, if I keep trying.

Beyond whatever constitutes the giddy compulsion of falling in love, there are at least two huge reasons to be drawn to women when you are a woman. One is Freudian and reinforces an essentialist picture of the sexes. In that Adrienne Rich—esque view, being with a woman provides comfort. She is like that first person you bonded with, the nurturer; through her you get the understanding, the seeming acceptance, the breast (well, *breasts*). The second reason is political: not just the seventies-era "How can I be a revolutionary when I'm in love with the enemy," but the more third-wave gloss of "Can I have a more satisfying, more equal relationship in which I like *myself* better with a woman?" That last aspect was a constant refrain with the women I interviewed, beginning with Anastasia:

> I specifically wanted to heal from a few mildly abusive sexual relationships I'd had with men as a teenager. And I just never again wanted to experience the creepy, exploitative sexual stuff I got throughout girlhood from grown men—strangers, family members, teachers. These experiences made me angry and afraid, which is a bad combination. So naturally I wanted to feel and be safer and smarter in relationships. I wanted to be loved more deeply and understood. I wanted to be with someone who would feel entirely at ease with my feminist worldview. And like everybody else in the world, I was attracted to people who I wanted to become. In my case: smart, self-assured, sexy, competent feminists. I was sure this kind of person did not exist in the shape of a man, and luckily I was attracted to women, so I chose to pursue women and presumed I would always choose women.

Bisexual women may not be more drawn to women than men—in Anastasia's case, she has dated mainly men since her breakup with the woman after me—but they often like *themselves* better with women than they do with men. I certainly do. I have yet to have that relationship with a man where I feel as strong and independent as I felt with the two serious female relationships I've had. When I think about why that might be, I realize that we were always talking, much like how I am always talking and connecting with my friends. I felt so understood. And with Amy especially, I always knew where I stood. We said "I love you" at the end of every phone conversation.

During the times I've been single, Anastasia has said, "I won't be jealous if you begin dating a man, but if you're with a woman . . ." Another friend, Kathryn Welsh, describes it as complete understanding with women—you feel you can read each other's mind. Kathryn founded Bluestockings feminist bookstore in New York in 1999 at the age of twenty-three, which is how we met, and she recently graduated from Harvard Business School. After several relationships with women, she is now involved with a man. "It has been a struggle to learn how it is that men relate to their emotions," she says.

> My last girlfriend and I had this crazy intense relationship—lots of talking and communicating. I just don't remember playing games with women. Now, with my boyfriend, I'll think, *Why doesn't he want to stay in the morning after breakfast?* You know, stay and have lunch and dinner and just continue to have fun? He's just up and out, and I'll talk to him a day or two later. Sometimes I look at him and feel like he's liberated—in fact, more liberated than me—by not having to obsess about our relationship. Other times I'll think it is sad that he is not as emotionally developed. He can't express himself that well. He constantly subverts his own feelings.

Deborah Tannen, a professor of sociolinguistics and the author of two bestsellers about how people communicate, refers to women as "intimacy junkies" and suggests that there are positive things to learn from men's physicality. In a 2006 interview in *Child* magazine, Tannen says that instead of talking, men "do"—and there can be healthy, non-verbal communication in having sex, playing tennis, or going to the game. Ironically, with women I am perhaps less autonomous, and that is what feels good to me. But there is total independence, and then there is being a good team, and the latter is what I'm always looking for and have yet to find with a man.

I remember very clearly the day I knew, just *knew* beyond the shadow of a doubt, that I would never live with the father of my child. It was months before I got pregnant. I was staying at his Brooklyn apartment for a week because a friend had relatives in town who were staying at my place. After a few days of calmly living among the ruins, I snapped. As he was off jogging one morning, I skated around shoeless on wet Swiffer pads trying to clean his uncleanable floors. I threw some bleach on the crumbly, corroded tile in the bathroom and began vacuuming the rest of the apartment like a madwoman. He walked in as I was trying to free the assorted bottle caps that had already jammed the vacuum (one false move under the couch yielded a bounty of recycling) and demanded to know what I was doing. I froze, caught in the act. As I put away the vacuum, my socks crunched over a fine scattering of debris. "As God is my witness," I hissed to myself, "I will not stand in cat litter again!"

Katha Pollitt, the poet and *Nation* columnist, wrote an essay in which standing in cat litter was a harbinger of relationship doom. In her case, it signaled that she and her lover had let things slide; they were no longer caring enough to live outside of the litter box. "I can be a pig around *her*," the gesture seemed to say. But I argue that living with men is often a constant battle to keep the litter box contained. My sister's husband has a Zenlike tolerance for walking on the stuff, while the sight of throw pillows gives him hives.

Soon after my son was born, my mother asked me if I

thought the next person I dated would be a man or a woman. My instinct was a man. I had been observing some of my friends in appealing-looking hetero partnerships with a yearning eye and I regularly referred to Ethan Hawke as my fake boyfriend, both because it seemed he was good with children and because of a series of coincidences that had put us on the same episode of Tina Brown's *Topic A*. However, when I actually thought about what I wanted from a partner, the person I pictured changed. Not all women want this, of course, but I want someone who knows how to make a bed and who agrees with me that even though it will just get messed up that night, it makes sense to straighten it anyway. I want someone who doesn't fear they are a "pussy" if I ask them to help me with an errand. I want someone who will go to the Seneca Falls Museum with me. I want someone with whom I can discuss my writing and who will be an intellectual muse. I want someone who will gossip about feminists with me. Apparently, I want a girlfriend. Or a wife. And I'm not the only one.

"Why I Want a Wife" is the name of a famous essay by a woman named Judy Syfers that appeared in the first is-sue of *Ms.* magazine in 1972. In nine succinct paragraphs, Mrs. Syfers outlines the job of wife, from working to send someone else to school to keeping track of the kids' sched-ules to creating and executing daily menu planning—basically, acting as an unpaid butler. When the essay was reprinted in the premiere issue of the ad-free *Ms.* in 1990, it was signed by Judy Brady. It turned out that she and Mr. Syfers had divorced. (He perhaps wanted a traditional wife who didn't write snotty essays; she reclaimed her maiden name.) I have a feeling that Mr. Syfers has a wife, while Judy Brady still does not, though at least she no longer has to *be* one.

The wife. Who wants to be her? Sure, there is a forty-five-billion-dollar wedding industry, but that's about brides, not wives. Many of my friends are married, but few of them cop to being wives—the selfless helpmeet whom Brady describes. In Anne Kingston's comprehensive exploration of that four-letter word, *The Meaning of Wife*, she opens the final chapter with a want ad:

> Employment opportunity: partnership opportunity in a venture known to have more than a 40 percent failure rate. You will fulfill a support role. Candidates must be attractive, cheerful, sociable, and organized. Responsibilities include domestic administration, entertaining, traveling, accompanying partner to professional events, and will often include reorganizing personal schedule at the last minute. Salary, vacation, sick leave, and pension to be determined by partner, and will be commensurate with the success or failure of venture. Performance to be evaluated at whim by partner. Position may require abandonment of education and/or career goals and is subject to termination at any time, without notice, by partner, even after thirty years of service. Severance to be determined by partner or the courts. No experience preferred.

Having a feminist consciousness helps to point out the unequal job sharing among husbands and wives, but the movement doesn't have any power to get men to actually divide chores more equally. Alix Kates Shulman even drew up a marriage agreement once she joined the women's liberation movement, hopeful that she could organize her household the way she could a meeting. The agreement was widely reprinted in settings from *Life* to *Redbook*, but Shulman wrote years later that it hadn't worked at all with her husband. In fact, despite "good intentions," his out-of-town business made it impossible for him to do half of the housework and child rearing.

Shulman did her revolutionizing from within a heterosexual marriage; others believed the ramparts were squarely outside. In the seventies, there was a profound fear of being gay, to be sure, but with the burgeoning understanding of sexism and misogyny, it became harder to understand why one would want to "sleep with the enemy," either. For some, lesbian love was a pragmatic route to fairness. (The sex and foot massages were just a bonus.)

"One thing that is different now is that women are better educated," said Susan Hull, a married copy editor in her forties, when I gave her the thumbnail sketch of *Look Both Ways* at a loud East Village club. "So that in addition to being friends and borrowing clothes, we can have an intellectual conversation and really learn from one another." In other words, we can get from women what another generation of women had to turn to men for. On the other hand, same-sex environments can feel limited and like a crutch for some women. They can imply a retreat to a fabulous utopia that gives you insight into the mainstream world; and they can also be a ghetto—even a literal one, since women make much less money than men.

In some ways, these issues are less obvious now than they were during the second wave. We have more access to equality than women did in the seventies, and men are different now, too. But, if anything, it seems that even more young women are looking both ways than ever before. Nerve.com personals bear this out, as do college campuses, on which I've spent a lot of time since 2000, when my first book, *Manifesta*, was published. Not only are feminist principles more blithely accepted nowadays, *USA Today* reports that gayness "no longer fazes most teenagers," citing a 1999 study commissioned by *Seventeen* magazine and the Kaiser Family Foundation. The study found that while in 1991, only 17 percent of teens said that they were comfortable with homosexuality, by 1999, more than half were. There are gay-straight alliances in forty-six states, and between 1998 and 2004, their number in high schools increased ten-fold, from two hundred to at least two thousand.[26] The an-nual "Young Hollywood" issue of *Vanity Fair* in 2002 featured nine up-and-coming screen sirens, including Selma Blair, Rosario Dawson, and Naomi Watts. Amid accompa-nying blurbs for each, the writer drooled about Blair's kiss with Sarah Michelle Gellar in *Cruel Intentions* and asked rhetorically of Naomi Watts in her role in *Mulholland Drive*, did "Grace Kelly ever have to maintain her poise during scorching lesbian love scenes?"

Bisexuality doesn't always feel solid, like a place we've landed where we can set up shop for a while. Sometimes it feels like an avenue to something, but it's not a path to a "real" or more stable heterosexual or gay life. It might be a way to a more honest life, one with more freedom for women. Perhaps its sense of flux—or the fact that it's best described more as a Tiresiasian story than a place—is due to the fact that men and women are in transition from our lim-ited roles of the past. Given the unfinished business of fem-inism, maybe no relationships have a real place to settle down. If you were married to a man for twenty-five years and then ran off with a woman, was the marriage a phase? "At times, home is nowhere. At times, one knows only ex-treme estrangement and alienation. Then home is no longer just one place. It is locations," writes bell hooks in her essay "Choosing the Margin as a Space of Radical Openness." "Home is that place which enables and promotes varied and ever-changing perspectives, a place where one discovers new ways of seeing reality."

There is some truth to all the clichés about places such as Smith College, the dressing room in strip clubs, softball teams, prisons, and convents being breeding grounds for women falling for each other. In the parlance of the paranoid, these environments encourage women to "go lesbian." Freud refers to these women as "contingent inverts," but a more modern notion of them would be that they are situational bisexuals. The idea is that the situation (no men around) provides the impetus for a woman to deviate from heterosexuality. However, with a little imagination and with feminism added, that Freudian value system shifts. The situation of *sexism* makes women constitutionally unable to feel completely satisfied in heterosexual relationships.

The situation of sexism has perverted women into thinking that they need a man in order to have any value in the world, so perhaps rather than asking if bisexuality exists, we should inquire how we even know what women truly desire? Do we know what we are really capable of, when men are so often the avenue to access, privilege, education, respect, and freedom? Today, many of the articles in magazines from *Jane* to the third-wave pop culture zine *Bitch* deal with the frustration that women feel with heterosexuality, given the real-life dynamics of inequality or drudgery. However, in no small part because of feminism's successes, many straight women now approach hetero relationships with what I think of as "gay expectations."

The journalist Meg Daly spoke of how feminism broadened her mind and oriented it toward women before she had any sexual relationships with women:

> In college I began being interested in women. I could be the poster child for all of those people who talk about how feminists turn everyone into lesbians—that was my story. I was taking Women's Studies classes, reading Adrienne Rich. I thought, *wow, there is this whole world of power that is open to me.* I was intellectually lesbian before I was physically. During college I really saw myself in lesbian politics, had some crushes on women, became friends

with lesbians, but I still dated guys. I didn't date women until after college.

For some, being with a woman resolved painful issues around being a woman, met needs that weren't likely to be met by a man. For instance, Gareth White, an actress and graduate student, felt like her first crush helped her deal with the constant critique she got from her family about her weight:

> I think I first knew I liked women when I developed this crush on a girl that I did theater with in high school. At first I thought that I just wanted to be friends with her, but then when I became friends with her I realized that I wanted to kiss her and was sexually attracted to her. She was older and had tons of confidence, no matter how false it was. The interesting part is that her mother is a lesbian and so she lived with her mother and her mother's partner, and I found this fascinating. She talked openly about questioning her sexuality, which I also thought was very cool.
>
> I was very unhappy in my life and in my skin at that point. To set the scene, I was and am overweight, I constantly fought with my mother and found little comfort in friends. I succeeded academically and planned rigorously how to get into an Ivy League school; it was the only thing that mattered to me. My parents pushed me academically and also pushed me to lose weight. I was signed up for programs and weighed and was, I have to say, abused a little by my mother about my weight. This girl I fell for wore strange clothes, was loud and obnoxious, I remember she was very nice to me but not very nice to everyone else.

Loving this girl who took up space allowed Gareth to accept herself a bit—and she could imagine doing this only with a woman, not a man. Gareth is bisexual, but I have found that having "gay expectations" in a heterosexual relationship is common among women raised after the second wave of feminism. More often than not, when Amy Richards and I lecture on a campus, we meet young women like Meredith Oosta, who told us: "I have high expectations of relationships." When I spoke to Meredith in 2003 she was a senior at Hope College, a small Christian school in Michigan. Meredith continued her list: "I want sexual fulfillment, emotional fulfillment, intellectual satisfaction. I think, why commit to someone if you don't have that?"

Why indeed? These women, some of them veterans of Women's Studies, are not expecting a world in which men ignore housecleaning or want to have sex with every morning erection; they're surprised if he insists she take his name once the kids are born. In the last thirty years, the whole of women's cultural condition has been challenged. Laundry strikes were staged; the orgasm was found, claimed, and defined by women; singleness was transformed from a tragedy into an identity, one with numerous TV shows centered on it. Men's roles have, of course, been affected by this—and in some ways, even redefined. Fathers are encouraged and expected to tap into deeper bonding with their children, to show emotion and love to their daughters *and* sons, to be home for the feedings, first steps, softball, and slumber parties. More men are, in fact, stay-at-home fathers. They are artists, often, whose more professional wives provide the salary and health insurance while the dads watch Elmo videos and go to Music Together class. But, taken as a whole, men aren't *that* different in the world. If working outside of the home, they still seem automatically to wrangle for higher salaries, as if they listened to Dale Carnegie tapes in utero, and are granted better pay as part of the male entitlement. Sure, women now share offices with men, but women still typically earn less (take an informal poll at about any workplace for proof). And those wives with the stay-at-home husbands? She is still usually the one who does the majority of the housework. According to Arlie Hochschild's *The Second Shift*, a study of households where both parents work, 61 percent of women still did almost all of the housework. Only 18 percent of men did half or almost half. That study came out in 1989. A decade later statistics about men's involvement in the second shift showed a steady gain (still dwarfed by women's share), followed by a slight decline.

High school girls are increasingly more open to the notion of cohabitation or children outside of marriage, according to a 1999 study from the National Marriage Project at Rutgers University. Add to this deglamorization of wifely duties how "normalized" same-sex relationships have become. Take Jackie Arcy and Jessica Hatem, for instance. I met Jackie and Jessica at their high school in suburban Ohio. They started a ChickLit class (by which they meant a class about feminism), which they then taught, and invited Amy Richards and me to address the students when we were nearby on a book tour. The next year they asked if they could spend some of their senior year of high school interning for us. One day I chatted with the two of them about being best friends and learned that they had "fooled around" for a year or so. Both were blithe about it. They kissed and made out during sleepovers and then, one day, Jackie decided she didn't want to anymore, so they stopped. Another young woman with whom I've worked, Constance DeCherney, twenty-three at this writing, doesn't consider herself bisexual, yet she described an intense same-sex relationship that, in a way, has yet to be surpassed.

> The first girl I ever enjoyed kissing was a best friend since elementary school. That relationship might have gone a lot further, had I not seen myself as straight. Both of us had the expectation that if we fell in love with a girl

we'd redefine our label. We had a deep attraction to one another but it was unclear what it was. If we were in a room together, it was as if there was no one else and there was a really weird week at the beach when we were kissing a lot.

Jackie and Jessica, as well as Constance, have had relationships—i.e., dates, I love you's—only with men, but it is interesting to me that they are so open and contemplative about their youthful fooling around. They aren't disturbed by it, and they take that attraction seriously. Perhaps it's the new openness about sexual shenanigans and the feelings girls have expressed since the invention of the sleepover that primes them for a vision of domestic harmony with men. Many women my age whom I interviewed speak of the deep love they felt for a woman who seems like their perfect match, except in gender. "I have a good friend from childhood who went to my college, too," says Meg Daly. "She was my soul mate, and she would have said that about me as well. My relationship with her, which was never sexual, was my training ground about how to be intimate."

Women are entering into relationships with men with gay expectations, but they don't know how to actualize those expectations or, sometimes, even acknowledge them. It's part of the paradox of feminism, of feminism's unfinished revolution: women expect equality from their relationships, but not from men. As a result, swinging toward women, who hold the same ideals about relationships, makes sense. Bethany Martin, another Hope College senior, put it like this: "If I could have equality and fulfillment with a woman, but I couldn't with a man—then why *wouldn't* I choose a woman?" In this way, then, bisexuality is a means to negotiate unequal relationships with men. It is a dialectic, a way of comparing what we do in relationships because that is "who we are," and what we do simply because it's easier than trying to get him to do it. Thus, looking both ways is a way to get information about ourselves, including clues to our passivity and complicity in sexism. This is a way that bisexuality subverts a dominant power and provides access to it, too.

I talked to Liza Featherstone about the freedom she felt with women, especially the freedom to be goofy:

> One thing I was getting from women was a greater blurring of the lines between friend and lover. I really think at that point I hadn't had men in my life who were friends-and-we-also-sleep-together. That was a big part of it, intimacy and silliness in a really great way. I was in a relationship with a man for a few years after I moved to New York City, and after we broke up I got in a very serious relationship with a woman for about four years. And I remember thinking one of those things I love about women is that you can have so much fun and be so silly in a way I had never found with men. I don't even know why that is. It doesn't seem like it would be a gender thing. Obviously a lot of relationships aren't lighthearted a lot of the time. They're broad in all kinds of ways, just like anything else.

My friend Ali called me while I was writing this chapter, disturbed and intrigued by a dream she'd had the night before. In it, she was having an affair with Ellen DeGeneres. This is a dream many gay or bisexual women have had—in my case, it's more of a daydream. But Ali is straight and has never even had the requisite fooling-around-with-a-friend, gayish experience. "I'm not attracted to Ellen or to women in general," she said, "but in this dream I felt so scared. I wasn't attracted to Ellen, but I also didn't want to lose her. I kept thinking how hard it was going to be to tell my mom. I felt such shock and shame and yet the idea of losing Ellen was even worse." As Ali's dream illustrates, even women who aren't looking both ways yearn subconsciously for a relationship they can imagine most clearly having with a woman.

Men, nowadays, often have gay expectations, too, having been raised as they were with feminism's ideals and a partial revolution in their roles. I can think of many reasons why straight men fall in love with bisexual women and lesbians. One is perceived inaccessibility, which interrupts the persistent image of the "trap" created by women's neediness. It also allows a man to throw himself into the relationship without fear that it will progress to the point of commitment. Then there is the reality: perhaps bisexual women and lesbians are more independent—at least in terms of their dependence on men. We are more likely to have shrugged off some of our female helplessness, fixed the car, because either there often was no man around to do it or we wanted to do it for our girlfriends. My fiftysomething lesbian friend K. was once in love with a married woman. Meanwhile, the woman's husband *adored* K. They talked baseball and boat maintenance.

Despite feminism's inroads, you see versions of preferring the company of one's own sex at heterosexual parties, where the men congregate around a game or in the living room and the women are gathered in the kitchen. In some way, my understanding of a bisexual identity props up unfair standards that feminists have fought to change. Bisexual women often date a man on the heels of a relationship with a woman. While her Sapphic past can challenge the male ego (Is he man enough to woo her from her lesbian life?), in other ways, it feeds into the idea that a woman should be great in bed (which usually comes from experience) without having had tons of male lovers. Men are threatened more by other men than by women. In *Chasing Amy*, Kevin Smith's 1997 film about a relationship between a straight man (Ben

Affleck) and a putative lesbian who turns out to have looked both ways (Joey Lauren Adams), this point is made manifestly clear. Ben Affleck's character finds out that his girlfriend, whose slutty behavior with girls right in front of him hadn't disturbed him at all, was also wild with men in high school. Upon learning this, he no longer loves or trusts her. "I hate to say it," says my baby's father, Gordon, "but half the reason bisexuality is so accepted among women is that men don't find it a problem." They find it hot. It's the oldest cliché in the book, hence the prevalence of girl-on-girl action in hetero porn. (Although I was certainly grateful for the trope when I began fooling around with Anastasia. It was too much of a leap to suddenly be gay, and this kind of male voyeurism served as a bridge to my physically relating to women.)

Men's "acceptance" of women's same-sex attraction contributes to its acceptance in the larger culture. Further, the fact that it is so unthreatening to men is due, in large part, to how unthreatening women are—and how invisible sex among women really is. It's unthreatening because it is perceived as either "for" the man's benefit or fundamentally dissatisfying, and thus could never replace intercourse. In another way, it plays into the virgin/whore dichotomy: she's so sexed up, she'll have sex with other women, but there is still that one man for her.

Nancy Friday, the second-wave chronicler of women's fantasies devoted a huge portion of her 1973 book *My Secret Garden* to what I would term bisexual desires. In a section titled "Women's Sexual Fantasies," Friday writes:

> However they handle this "other" side of their sexual nature, in fantasy or in relating it to reality, I have found women to be remarkably candid in discussing their erotic imaginings of other women . . . Some women . . . introduce a man into their fantasies of other women; the

bisexuality makes it more acceptable. For the same reason, as with Celia, the other woman is sometimes made anonymous. Or the fantasist emphasizes that she is totally passive with the other women. Or simply is watching other women and not involved herself.

Conversely, as straightforward with me as women have been in discussing their sexual thoughts of other women, and as accepting of themselves for having them, their men have been just the opposite in regard to their own homosexual thoughts. Women say that their descriptions of their own erotic fantasies of other women may even bring a fond smile to their lover's lips; homoeroticism between women seems to be acceptable to men, and indeed is often a sexual turn-on. But any suggestion that the man might have these same feelings about other men is treated as an insult or a threat. It's one thing for women to have these kinds of thoughts, but quite another (ugly, dirty) for a man.

Irritating or diminishing though it is, I don't think men's prurient interest in watching undermines the value of women making love to other women. And sex is just one of the many things that go into a relationship, same sex or otherwise. But when I try to parse what women think of their relationships, I often hear, "It's about love," meaning it's not sullied by politics or strategic decisions. Falling in love is about love, but relationships are about other things often, things such as comfort, support, and security, both emotional and material. Women nowadays have been raised to expect much more for themselves, indeed, to expect a "partner." The problem is we don't necessarily expect more from men. (Of course, this is a problem only for those who *want* to have relationships with men.) Bisexual women may have taught themselves to expect just a bit more than they otherwise would have. "I think that after you have been with women, there are a lot of men and a lot of things men do that you would never settle for," Liza Featherstone told me. "You wouldn't be with a man who couldn't talk about his feelings in an informed and subtle way. On just the most obvious level, you would never be with a man who wouldn't go down on you."

CHAPTER 6

BUT IS IT SEX?

Bisexual women tend to have Venus in Gemini.

—Ophira Edut, astrologist and coauthor of *Astrostyle: Star-Studded Advice for Love, Life, and Looking Good*

My lover happens to be a man, but the sex we have is perty damn queer, and we love all of our toys.

—Ani DiFranco, from an interview with me, September 22, 1997

I lost my virginity at age twenty to a classmate I saw on and off for most of my college career. Although he was kind of a cheaterly scoundrel (a charismatic sex addict à la Bill Clinton), I really liked him. He was a great person to have as a first lover (very experienced, with the chiseled physique of a long-distance runner, and a great kisser) and I had waited to have sex, so it was consensual and a positive emotional experience. Physically, though, it was not orgasmic or even pleasurable, really. I remember worrying for a second that I was having anal sex, the pressure in that area was so intense. My friend Marianne also lost her virginity that year, and we laughed hysterically about the anal confusion. (Giving birth to Skuli fourteen years later elicited a similar sensation. My father, a doctor, pointed out to me that when something that large is in your vagina, it puts quite a bit of pressure on your rectum.) I don't mean that I didn't enjoy that first foray into intercourse—in fact, I had a smile on my face for days afterward and loved the new feeling in my body of having done it *finally*. Moreover, I was very attracted to the guy, and we had fooled around intensely for months leading up to having sex, and slept together for years after.

Still, in those three years with that college beau I never once came close to having an orgasm. I've had half a dozen male lovers since him, and most have tried industriously to make me come, but still, no orgasm (at least none without the help of a battery-powered implement). But with Anastasia, I had my first orgasm about three weeks after we began sleeping together; with Amy Ray, the learning curve was even faster. To recap: sex with women is orgasmic; sex with men is occasionally orgasmic, and intercourse has yet to be orgasmic for me. "Intercourse isn't orgasmic?" a bisexual friend, currently engaged in a white-hot lesbian affair, asked me after reading that admission. "It isn't for me, either—doesn't that make us gay?"

When it came to learning about sex, I believe I am typical for my age. By the age of ten, I had scanned *Our Bodies, Ourselves* for the parts about masturbation and rolled around naked with the neighbor girl, pretending to be her husband as I planted little pecks all over her freckly neck and shoulders. Initially, I had tried and failed to be the wife—who, we decided, was the kissee, not the kisser—but it tickled. My other pre-libido pastime was suiting up in my white beaded two-piece (which I called my "string bikini," as if I were Bo Derek) and playing a game I referred to as cowboys and Indians, but was really more akin to *Charlie's Angels*. According to that game, I was a scantily clad Indian princess, and the boy from across the street was an aggressive cowboy. He had to chase me, capture me as I struggled and kicked, and throw me in "jail," which was the inflatable pool in his backyard. I loved that game.

I was reading *Cosmo* one day and zipping through the latest Judy Blume book the next. Like many of her readers, I read the Blume books that were "age-inappropriate"—*Forever* in fourth grade, *Wifey* in sixth. All I remember of the latter is someone's husband going through the hamper at a party and sniffing some panties—unbelievably perverse to my mind back then. In *Forever*, the protagonist's boyfriend, Michael, names his penis "Ralph," permanently ruining that name and also creating one of the friendliest depictions of a phallus I would encounter in my many years of feminist scholarship. From Judy Blume's *Then Again, Maybe I Won't*, I learned that men ejaculate. From *Forever*, I learned that it occasionally gets on your stomach and has to be wiped up with Kleenex. In general Blume schooled me in a whole affable code for dirty things I wanted to know about but that also intimidated me. All of the *P* words: periods, pubic hair, panty sniffers, and, most of all, penises.

Ms. Blume might have taught me a lot, but before I ever saw a man's body, I saw women in *Playboy*. From the late 1960s to the early 1970s my father kept a stash of them in our basement laundry room. Later they were moved to the garage. As a child, I led expeditions into the garage to unveil Miss November 1967 or any of her playmate sisters. They, too, were dirty yet affable. A dozen years later, at *Ms.*, where the founder's fame had grown from her exposing the Playboy Bunny life (essentially eight hours of poorly paid sexual harassment), I interviewed Miss July 1956, Alice Denham, and learned that the mastermind behind those friendly images, Hugh Hefner, actually did expect sex if one appeared in his pages. Denham also confided to me that he was often impotent, which struck me as poetic justice. But back in my own garage girlie show, *Playboy* was not about Hef. I didn't even know who he was. It certainly wasn't about the incredible articles and interviews my dad claimed he subscribed to it for. No, *Playboy* was about breasts. And *Playboy* was for everyone—girls as well as boys, especially when it came to preteens exploring their nascent sexuality.

I grew up with an intimate idea of what a woman's body was like. I stared at models constantly and I stared at my own body, too. I even went through a phase, at about age ten, when I was sure I wanted to be a stripper and would practice taking off my nightie in front of the mirrored door of my shower. Women, many of whom turn out straight and many of whom turn out gay, study women's bodies, just as men do. And we all have plenty of opportunities to do so, in bus ads, magazine covers, and increasingly easy-to-access actual porn. "I believe that one of the major reasons that we latch on to racy stories and sexual images is that we use them, consciously or unconsciously, to measure ourselves," writes sociologist Meredith F. Small. "The photographs, the stories, and the headlines are comparative devices for an important question—Am I normal?"

Bisexuality—or, in this case, having sex with women when you have had sex with men—serves a similar function of answering the question "Am I normal?" The insecurity that many women feel about their bodies—Is it gross to go down on me? Is my vagina bizarre looking? Do I get *too* wet?—is ameliorated somewhat by having sex with (and loving) a body that is like your own. Melissa Dessereau, a thirty-six-year-old social worker and friend, told me she was drawn to women for years, but afraid that the sex would turn her off. "I'd had this sense like, 'I wonder what it's like to go down on a woman. Can I hang with that?' I had enough internal misogyny that I worried," she recalls. "Once I found out that it was perfectly fine, I was like, 'Oh, I can do this!' After sex that first time, I felt like I could be with women for real."

But it's not just the self-esteem-building aspects that draw women to women. Some of the allure is just the opposite: the illicitness of a forbidden love. Nancy Friday's *My Secret Garden* details these outré sexual trysts. Often, men are involved, either as voyeur or participant, but in a way that is directed by the woman who is having the fantasy. Men "wanting to watch" or wanting men to watch is generally critiqued as undermining the validity of this kind of sexual experience. This critique is most often leveled at high-school-age girls whose same-sex public smooches and fooling around is written off as a performance for boys. This ignores the fact that a lot of what girls (and boys) do in high school sexually isn't totally authentic—it is, in a way, a performance of what they think sexually active adults do. These young women, or at least some of them, are getting more than male attention through their experiments with women. Debbie Grossman, now a twentysomething photographer in New York, recalls her early sexual experiences:

> I'd read my mom's romance novels for the sex scenes, and that was really exciting for me, starting in seventh grade. But I remember sitting in Latin class one day, and I was thinking, I am *never* gonna have sex for *so* long, and how am I gonna deal with that? And that was thinking about boys. But by the next year, I was totally in love with my friend Laura. We were gonna run off to Athens, Georgia, to hang out with REM, and I consciously had sex feelings about her, because she wore way too much perfume. We snuck into this rated R movie, and I remember seeing this sex scene, and smelling her, and I just wanted to say, "Oh my god, Laura, you're driving me crazy." Laura had this picture of Laura Dern framed next to her bed, and we were all obsessed with *Twin Peaks*. I was definitely interested in lesbians on TV. I was like, "I wonder if Laura is a lesbian?" I was going on thirteen then.

The desires of teenaged girls, such as Debbie during her sexual awakening, tend to be written off if they are directed at women or girls. It's true that at that age our sexuality is in the process of emerging and we are having some of our first forays, but same-sex experimentation is hardly any less (or more) thought out than opposite-sex trysts. We fumble as we learn about sex. When Liza Featherstone began sleeping with men, for instance, it wasn't because she had found someone with whom to make evolved and meaningful love. She had attended a high school for very smart kids, whom she categorized as highly undersexed. By college, at the University of Michigan, "it was just time," Liza says. "It was so boring not to have it." She continues:

> When I finally did have sex, it was not with a person I cared about that much. I was dating him, but, honestly, I didn't feel like the standard had to be really high. It was my first time and I was like, I want to get this over with. I dated a number of really unmemorable men. The first guy I had sex with was Republican, and we met at the union. He was a Republican punk rocker—totally, on the whole, an obnoxious person. I didn't really care. I was like, I'm ready. It was not satisfying sexually. I could see how sex could be really great but that was not. It wasn't so bad that I was like, why do people think this is a big deal? I don't know what my understanding was of why it wasn't great. I assumed that it had something to do with the fact that I wasn't comfortable with him and I kind of fundamentally didn't like him.

Meg Daly also had lackluster first sexual experiences with men. She describes her discovery of women as her sexual awakening:

> I began to learn about my own body as I learned about feminism. I didn't know how to get any pleasure for my-self until I was twenty. That was when I learned how to masturbate. A bunch of women in my feminist group were talking about it and they handed me Lonnie Barbach's *For Yourself*. Until then, I had this split personality. I was really strong and assertive in certain ways, but a

wallflower in other ways; certainly I was passive about
sexual gratification. I somehow had learned to just lie
there, basically. Up until I learned how to pleasure myself, I used sex as a vehicle for some emotional need. I
was definitely learning about my own body and pleasure
when I became interested in women's bodies. I wasn't
scared of my own body anymore, so suddenly other
women's bodies seemed intriguing, not scary. I mean,
bless feminism. If I believed in God I'd say, "God bless
feminism."

Or put a different way, in what I think of as Baumgardner
Girl logic (Woody Allen–esque chronic disappointment),
my sister Jessica told me, "I think this bisexuality stuff has a
lot to do with sex. There are so many girls not having good
sex with men. They think, 'My God, a girl would have to be
at least as good as that guy was.' "

When Helen Gurley Brown was head of *Cosmo*, her office
deviated from the beige neutrality of the surrounding editorial cubicles at Hearst Magazines. Leopard spots carpeted
the floor, upon which sat darling faux Louis the Something
chairs, glass tables covered with New Age crystals, and
salmon-colored fabric flocked with bright flowers decorated
the windows and love seat. The walls were padded and covered in pink material, giving the effect that you were sitting
inside a healthy vagina. When I visited, Mrs. Brown was
seated behind a large desk talking on the phone, flanked by
her trusty old typewriter. She *hates* technology.

The date of my visit was July 18, 1997. HGB, then
seventy-five, was wearing a glittery Lurex-threaded baby
blue short-sleeve mini dress, no stockings, and taupe shoes,
and breasts far perkier than mine. Normally, I wouldn't say
that you wear your breasts, but she did—new breast im-
plants that she had gotten at age seventy-three. "I'm an ardent feminist," she told me. "In fact, I'd say with a lot of

feminist ideas I got there first and a lot earlier. But some of
their ideas were just wrong."

Like what? I asked.

"Like saying that objectification is terrible. Sometimes it's
wonderful!"

Her words gave me pause. Was she right? Should we stop
worrying and dive into objectification? "From childhood on,
American boys and girls learn to identify sexual feelings
with the only images available to them: the Guess girls,
Cindy Crawford, Budweiser babes," writes Ellen Garrison in
Bitch: A Feminist Response to Pop Culture. Garrison goes on to say
that though she is "rampantly heterosexual," there were still
many "years before I viewed a male body in a sexual light,
the most direct visual correlation to those unspoken 'sexy'
feelings has been the objectified woman we all know and
loathe."

It seems to me that the objectified woman has indeed
been critiqued. And like other expressions of idealized femininity—from Barbie to baking—pointing out how unreach-
able Barbie's figure was became as normal as pointing
out stars in the sky to seventies feminists. My generation,
roughly speaking, grew up with both Budweiser babes and
the feminist critique of Budweiser babes. In short, growing
up with feminism has the effect of defanging the babe.

The fact of feminism has created a space for women to
appreciate women's bodies openly—others and their own.
The fact of feminism has also made it possible for women to
imagine inhabiting any role or space men inhabit, including
the one that involves "objectifying." Part of feminists' critique of the sexpot we know and loathe is not simply that
we might compare ourselves, as Naomi Wolf points out in
The Beauty Myth, and be made "to feel ugly in sex." It is also
that there didn't used to be a role for women to take in order to participate in the sexual market of desire-and-be-
desired—*except* for the position of the passive "objectified

one." That has changed because of feminists, but Bisexual women are a huge part of what is being called the pro-sex feminist movement. Susie Bright, Carole Queen, and Michelle Tea are just a few of the luminaries who have absorbed the critique of objectification without feeling guilt about their sex lives.

As women protested being reduced to sex objects, the healthy and titillating aspects of objectification were tossed out with the sexism. Is the fact that men tend to watch and women are aroused by watching themselves get watched (here I'm paraphrasing John Berger, who created the term "the male gaze") necessarily negative? For years I feared I'd never have a friendly relationship with a penis (as my therapist phrased it)—largely because I was so insecure about fumbling, I couldn't just explore. It wasn't until I began dating a woman who was very interested in penises and who imagined me with men that my fear of the phallus began to change. My interest was mediated or enhanced by another person's desires, but because she was a woman, I felt that I was a part of the sexual transaction, too—I became a player, not just an object. Dating women altered my view of porn, too, providing a place where I could be a viewer and not worry that I was being exploited or that my partner saw all women as blow-up sex dolls. In her Broadway show *I'm Still Here, Damnit!* Sandra Bernhard provides one of my favorite examples of objectification. She pages through a J.Crew catalogue, but says she's shopping not for new cargo pants—but for a new girlfriend.

One of the many unintended consequences of feminism is that it didn't get rid of women's need to be noticed by the more powerful—in fact, I'd argue that we all (male, female, and points in between) harbor this need. Feminism just opened up that power position to women, too. By valuing women—as smart, successful, daring, sexy, rich, or creative—we pine for *their* attention and get the familiar jolt of sexual excitement from it, just as we did (and do) from men. Feminists had hoped that the addictive nature of objectification ("God, you're gorgeous") would be ameliorated by women's rise in status ("There *is* more to life than being a sex object!"). But the pleasure of being objectified—thought beautiful, sexy, special, and captivating—was drastically underplayed by feminists.

Walking down East Third Street in late April 2002, I caught sight of myself in a car window. I looked awful, but the kind of awful that can almost be beautiful. My hair was dirty and a mess, my skin was pale, and I could see dark circles raccooning my eyes, but the effect struck me as delicate—Meryl Streep in *Sophie's Choice*, after she has made it to Brooklyn. I thought about how Amy Ray would have looked at me on such a day and said, "You look beautiful right now," and how Gordon would probably say the same. Both imagined judgments made me feel pretty and romantically in love. I feel much more at ease with my desire for attention than I did in college, when I was first learning about the "male gaze." The problem wasn't being sexy or objectified, it was getting to be *only* sexy or an object—and having your worth derived solely from that. Moreover, it was being excluded from the realm of the objectifiers, not having that taste of male privilege. Obviously there is a singular pleasure in being looked at and appreciated for your sex appeal. If that weren't the case, transsexual or transgendered people would not be willing to give up potential physical sexual pleasure in the form of a functioning clitoris or penis in order to live as another gender.

In 1972, in the famed first issue of *Ms.*, Anselma Dell'Olio declared that "The Sexual Revolution Wasn't Our War."[27] The 1960s had brought the Pill (a quantum leap forward in reliable birth control, though ushering in STDs as men threw away their condoms, and infertility as untreated STDs wreaked havoc on reproductive plumbing), an end to

pointy bras and oppressive girdles, and a new openness
about premarital sex. But the sexual revolution failed to be
pro-woman in its application. The reins were firmly in
male hands and Hugh Hefner–style swinging bachelors
were carving out a new context in which their casual-to-
predatory sexual proclivities could flourish, even in polite
company. That fact is one reason why Helen Gurley
Brown's narratives of females having sex outside of marriage
were so significant, and why Ani DiFranco's music became
so powerful a generation or two later. DiFranco's songs were
full of women's fantasies: dreams of fighting back against
molesters, of picking up a guy for a one-night stand, of
bleeding in the dull corporate boardroom and marking the
space as female, and of getting together with an exciting
girl. DiFranco described genuine sexual freedom. Meanwhile, the sexual revolution meant, in Dell'Olio's words,
that, "in truth, women had been liberated only from the
right to say no to sexual intercourse with men." She
continues:

> And as often as we repeat the following story, it never
> seems to be enough: According to Ovid, Tiresias, the
> blind prophet of Thebes who had been both a man and a
> woman, was asked to mediate in a dispute between Jove
> and Juno as to which sex got more pleasure from love-
> making. Tiresias unhesitatingly answered that women
> did. Two thousand years and several sexual revolutions
> later, we still believe the opposite to be true.

As Dell'Olio's two-pronged argument suggests, second-
wave feminists were advocating both for freedom from un-
wanted sex as well as for orgasms and sexual satisfaction.
Their legacy, sadly, has been flattened to emphasize their
protest of the sexual exploitation of women, just as "V-Day"
performances of *The Vagina Monologues* (bisexual feminist Eve

Ensler's successful play, which celebrates sexual pleasure as much as it fights violence) are interpreted as dealing mainly with victimization.

Despite the fact that feminists are as diverse as women are, feminism doesn't have a likewise reputation. Individual women are often sucker-punched when they find out that taking on the label of feminist may instantly transform them in the view of the world at large from single sexpot into dour spinster. These unsuspecting feminists are shocked by it, you can tell, especially since the addition of feminism often marks a personal journey to becoming sexually awakened. Perhaps that is why every few years or so male lifestyle writers discover "pro-sex feminists," rare birds with highly unusual behavior for feminists (according to these writers), behavior such as heterosexuality and smiling. The most famous example of extolling pro-sex feminists was the 1993 *Esquire* profile of a handful of third-wave-ish writers, including Naomi Wolf, bell hooks, and Rebecca Walker, which dubbed them the "Do-Me feminists." The article evoked a flurry of critique and near obsession in me. But, looking back, I think the response reflected the confusion about what feminism's significant critiques of sex and male-female dynamics meant for women.

Because feminists, particularly second-wave feminists, created a language for violence against women, we feel some odd sense of oppression about sex that comes not from religion or Freud or misogyny, but from our own movement. It's as if when feminism was reignited, it released some scowling feminist chaperone who pokes around in our daily lives, always exhorting us to think of the big picture—female emancipation. The chaperone might point out that without equality, romance and orgasms are hardly worth your while. This sense that someone is judging us is why it feels normal to declare that one is pro-sex, to distinguish oneself from that bogey feminist who never wants to have a date or get laid. For hip second-wavers this bogey feminist was Susan B. Anthony; for us hip third-wavers, the buzz kill is often boiled down to the second wave.

This paranoid description does not accurately represent the history or full sentiment of the second wave, of course. The second wave gave us a wide range of thought on sex—from anti-porn and rape crisis activists to myriad sex liberationists. Both Gloria Steinem and Alix Kates Shulman point out that they managed to be tarred with the brush of sexlessness *and* the brush of sluttiness. In truth, at meetings I attend hosted by second-wavers, they often seem more concerned with sexual liberation—and more turned off by traditional or gay marriage—than I am. As discussed earlier, one influential feminist (and lesbian), Anne Koedt, broadcast the importance of the clitoris to women's orgasms, while another, Shere Hite, conducted a nationwide study of female sexuality from a feminist perspective. In 1970, Hite was a graduate student in sociology at Columbia University. To make money, she picked up work as a hand model, and among the gigs was an ad for Olivetti typewriters. When the ad finally ran, she was humiliated to see that the copy under the photo read, "The typewriter that's so smart, she doesn't have to be." Outraged at unwittingly promoting the dumb secretary stereotype, she headed to Olivetti headquarters only to encounter a group of women from NOW already protesting the ad.

That moment was Hite's introduction to the women's movement, and she soon became one of its lasting stars. Her graduate project was a nationwide study of female sexuality—and not as an afterthought second volume (as with Kinsey), nor passive women headshrunk by brilliant men (as with Freud). Hite asked "3,000 women, ages 14 to 78, to describe in their own words their most intimate feelings about sex," and that became her 1976 bestseller *The Hite Report.* Hite amplified women's voices, letting them describe their own sex lives.

At *Ms.*, when I was first learning any sort of queer vocabulary, I frequently put my foot in my mouth. One day, I asked my witty lesbian cubicle mate, Julie Felner, when she had "lost her virginity." "Which one?" she asked. "With a man or a woman?" "Oh, both," I lied. "I meant both, of course." In truth, I meant men. She blew my mind, actually, by suggesting that having sex with a woman shared qualities with, you know, *real* sex. My mind was abuzz, but I was too embarrassed to ask her what losing her virginity to a woman meant. Years later, I would definitely say that I am no virgin when it comes to sex with women, yet it would be hard for me to put my finger on exactly when that deflowering happened. During Anastasia, of course—but when I had my first orgasm? The first time we both had them in the same session? Oral sex? This effective scissoring thing that we used to do with our legs that made crucial parts of our bodies connect? My mind was stuck in barely contemplated received wisdom, thinking about virginity in terms of breaking a hymens when I knew that many women lose their hymen to horseback-riding or a tampon.

I think my lack of clarity points to Shere Hite's hopefulness about women completing the sexual revolution. Today, as thirty years ago, there is a gap between what gives women pleasure and what we call real sex. *Real* sex can lead to pregnancy. *Real* sex requires birth control. *Real* sex (and now I'm channeling seventh-grade health class) is when a man and a woman love each other very much and the man slips his penis into her vagina (why is it always "slips"?). There is an allure to the kind of sex that can lead to pregnancy. The stakes are high, and that is racy and powerful, even if not, in my case, orgasmic. And sex with women is powerful in a different way and lends itself, in my case, to more easily accessible sexual pleasure.

If I had to locate a frame for all of my sexual repression, I don't think it would be anything as strong sounding as sexism. It's more subtle. I don't feel that sex makes you dirty—or I do, but I think that's a good thing. My understanding of Christianity (the religion in which I was raised) doesn't condemn premarital sex. I think about sex a lot, so I have some version of a libido—and yet I am highly repressed. The force organized against me is fear of embarrassment. I like to be in control and to know what I am doing, and sex doesn't always work that way. Perhaps one could boil that down to insecurity—as in I need self-esteem—or a lack of trust in myself or in men.

Trust was the sexual clincher for Dolores Alexander, the once-married early NOW member from chapter 3. "Once I had had sex with a woman," says Alexander,

> it was mind-blowing, it was so much better than with men. [My sexuality] just never became a question, I just stayed there. The issue was trust. I felt that I could trust women so much more than I ever could trust a man. You are dealing on a truly peer level with women and you are not with men—or at least I wasn't.

But even if that is true, many women still want something particular from men. I asked Ani DiFranco if there was anything she missed from guys when she was with a girl. "Well," she said,

> dick. But it's hard to generalize about genders, because I also feel like I am only just now awakening to my body *really*. Like going down on a person: I was never really comfortable with that being done to me. I suddenly felt

like I was onstage again, which is not what I want in that moment. And there was always this kind of pressure that would set in, where I am supposed to perform and make the other person feel good. So, I think that got in the way with women—and got in the way of me finding a satisfying place to be lovers with the women I was with. I was thirty-one before I was able to have an orgasm with somebody going down on me. Whatever my sexuality was when I first met it, it's a much different creature now then it was then. And I imagine that it's going to be much different in the future, too.

I asked Liza Featherstone if she felt she learned specific things from dating men that she was able to bring to her sexual relationship with a woman.

Something I definitely got from being with men was a sense that, for a lot of women only dating women, it takes longer to arrive at the decision that you really want sex to be aggressive. I think you get there eventually. I mean, everyone wants to be in some kind of aggressive sexual situation. When I first started having sex with women, I remember thinking, "I really like this but I kind of want to be a little more attacked and objectified." And I think most lesbians do want that, or they want to be at some end of that.

In 1994, I worked on the sex issue of *Ms.* The editorial meetings were really raucous, with one editor mentioning how she used food in crazy oral sex encounters with her man and another saying how she loved to get her whole face wet when making love to a woman. My somewhat sex-less contribution was mentioning that I didn't know how to have an orgasm. My point was that I had been raised with *Our Bodies, Ourselves* and all of the Judy Blume books—and even less nutritious sexual cues, such as *The Blue Lagoon* and *Playboy*. But I didn't necessarily know my own body. And I actually felt kind of sheepish that I didn't. I should know better, right? It's the paradox of feminism: Women raised with its benefits feel like chumps when we still get accidentally pregnant or can't have an orgasm. "We are part of a generation of women that likes to promote ourselves as really independent—go-getters," says Meg Daly. "Some of that is true, but I have to say I have had a harder time exploring those gray areas, the places where I am feeling insecure."

Bisexuality can reveal unasked questions about sex. My way of compensating for sexual insecurity—the openness that intimacy needs—was performing. If I was a vixen, my partner's pleasure proved my power but allowed me to remain fuzzy and perplexed about my own pleasure. Gordon once described an ex of his as having a very "practiced" blow job, one with the hand and the mouth and the big hair all swinging around. It took me a moment to realize that he didn't think of it as a good thing. "Men provide a really good example of how to enjoy yourself sexually, because they pretty much enjoy sex," says Liza Featherstone. "They're pretty much expressing their desires, and I think women should take that as an example. I was always conscious of being pleased." I felt that way with Anastasia and Amy—a little more awake to my own desires and pleasures, in part because I was less sure of how to perform. That role that many women learn almost from childhood didn't obviously apply. "Robin was *pret à manger*," is how Jonathan Franzen describes the ease with which Denise was able to come with Robin after the years of eye-squinting focus it took to have orgasms with her husband. "You didn't need a recipe to eat a peach."

My first night in bed with Gordon, it had been almost five years since I had been around a penis in any appreciable way and his seemed bizarrely large to me. I looked down and then said, "Um, your penis is really big." He glanced at me to see if it was a practiced remark and then replied, "It's not, actually."

"Oh." I paused and then smiled. "I don't really know what I'm doing." And it was one of the most genuine sexual moments I have ever had. And we fumbled on.

CHAPTER 7

MEN: CAN'T LIVE WITH THEM . . .

The male body is ground and shelter to me . . . When it is maligned categorically, I feel as if my homeland is maligned.

—Naomi Wolf, from her 1993 book
Fire with Fire

Gross.

—Jennifer Baumgardner, 1993,
in response to above quote

When men in my life have confronted me about my feminist beliefs, they often point out that feminism is presupposed in some way on generalizations that tar most men unfairly. "You talk as if all women have been raped and all men are rapists," male friends and foes at my college would often say to me, "and *I'm* not a rapist." "Right!" another would join in. "And *I'm* not barring you from jobs, *I'm* not battering my wife, *I'm* not keeping anyone down!" Put that way, my arguments against sexism seemed mythic—a feeling, a delusion, even—rather than something specific. My responses were often inadequate: "One in four women is raped, though," I'd counter, feeling trapped but eyeing them suspiciously nonetheless. "*Someone* is doing those assaults." Years later, I wonder why feminist language penetrated me so quickly? (Of course, back in college I never would have used the word *penetrate*.) It made such sense on a gut level. Why did I have that feeling that men were predatory and out to get me?

In part it's because from earliest girlhood, in minor and often vague ways, men have sniffed around me, as if stalking dinner—starting with the boy who always touched my

Jordache-covered butt on the bus in sixth grade to the socially retarded loner who used to hang out in the deserted
downtown shopping mall where I worked, buying me cheap
chocolates and generally making me feel uncomfortable.
The attention made me feel self-conscious and nervous, and
yet it also felt like power and an affirmation that I was attractive. In fact, I'd almost say I allowed the butt-grabber to
touch me. In most cases, though, I felt a pretty clear repul-
sion for these guys, and yet found it nearly impossible to be
straight with them that I wasn't interested or that they were
bothering me. I was often worried that I had somehow misread the situation and didn't want to be rude. So even if
I felt powerfully alluring in those moments, the tongue-
tiedness left me feeling weak. My way of getting some
space was to complain about these men behind their backs:
the bus kid was a lecherous perv; the mall guy was a lame
stalker. If it's hard to tell men whom you *don't* like what you
don't want, it is probably also hard to tell men you do like
what you do want.

A few years ago I received an award from the Common-
wealth Club. At the event, held in San Francisco, the inter-
viewer asked me about this book. I said one of its goals was
to address if women who looked both ways learned from
women how to get what we wanted from a relationship—
information that we could, if inclined, use to have more satisfying and equal relationships with men. "Could I have the
relationship I had with Amy with the men I date?" I asked.
"Or maybe not with the men *I* date"—everybody laughed—
"but, theoretically, could a woman achieve this?"

In a way, I was just going for the laugh by exempting myself from the goal, but in another way, the joke points to a
crucial challenge in creating equality: If we point out what
men do wrong in general, does that mean we know how to
ask for what we want in our relationships or that we would

even risk asking for it? Are women a big part of the problem?

"Women's second class position in patriarchal culture is painfully reflected in their psychology," the feminist therapists Luise Eichenbaum and Susie Orbach have written in their book *Understanding Women*. "Women do not feel whole; women do not feel confident in themselves; women feel less than equal; women feel like children, not adults; women feel powerless; women feel overdependent; women feel passive; women feel imprisoned by their anger and by the clouds of depression that often surround them." In Eichenbaum and Orbach's women-only therapy group, they noted, "the feelings of being second class, of being invalid within a group," diminished.

Toward the end of my relationship with Amy Ray, I was in my early thirties, and I was more committed than I had ever felt before. It was also the most mutually supportive relationship I had ever had. Unlike Anastasia, Amy didn't seem oppressed by me, as if only one of us could be creative at a time. Unlike Steven, Amy loved to go to gay marriage rallies (and WTO protests, and actions against the School of the Americas, and the Veteran Feminists of America Conference, and . . .). So it was good. But I wondered if I could have what I had with her—down to the orgasms and great phone calls—with a guy. At first, the question was hypothetical, but as our schedules and lifestyles headed in distinctly different directions (I was always on the West Coast when she was touring on the East; she loves the Georgia countryside while I fled smalltown America to be in places like New York)—and when I met Gordon—the question became real.

It is a question that many of the women I interviewed for this book have asked themselves. Could I be this way with a man? Could I have this self-respect, autonomy, and support with a man? Dolores Alexander, the second-waver and early NOW member, describes her transformation in terms of fleeing oppressive male figures. By extension, she understands her relationship to men in a larger casing: the huge, all-purpose frame of patriarchy.

> My marriage was like being with my father. My husband was very demanding and organized and intellectual. In those days, I saw myself as disorganized and lacking direction. He always knew where he wanted to go and he also dictated what was required of me. I had to work—that was expected—but I also had to do all of the wifely duties, like laundry and cleaning. I rebelled subconsciously. I kept losing his socks—one at a time. Everything I did for him was a duty or responsibility. Everything he did for me was a favor. This was before the women's movement, of course.
>
> One time, I was running late and I was so frightened to go home. I knew he was going to be angry with me. I thought to myself, "This has to change. I can't be frightened to go home and fear that this guy will in some way punish me." It was in moments like that . . . I began to realize that I had to get out.

For women's liberation movement veterans like Alexander, Valerie Solanas's unhinged *SCUM Manifesto* can be read as fact rather than satire. (In her 1972 memoir, Simone de Beauvoir refers to the *SCUM Manifesto* as a classic in the mode of Jonathan Swift.) Solanas began the 1967 treatise by declaring, "Life in this society being, at best, an utter bore and no aspect of society being at all relevant to women, there remains to civic-minded, responsible, thrillseeking females only to overthrow the government, eliminate the money system, institute complete automation, and destroy the male sex." The reason her manifesto had such frisson, though (besides Solanas's shooting Andy Warhol the year before it was published) was that there was tremendous rage toward men in that day—rage that was just beginning to find outlets. This righteous anger eventually had one justification: stopping men from exerting power over women. As stated by the radical second-wave group Redstockings, "We identify the agents of our oppression as men . . . Men have controlled all political, economic and cultural institutions and backed up this control with physical force. They have used their power to keep women in an inferior position. *All men* receive economic, sexual and psychological benefits from male supremacy. *All men* have oppressed women."

I absorbed that line of reasoning almost as soon as I hit college. For my generation, understanding patriarchy was eminently useful, too, but for a much shorter period of time—a stage of development, even, one might say, like puberty. I learned about recent feminist history in college, and the term *patriarchy* was key to making visible things such as date rape or the preponderance of men in fields of study such as philosophy and mathematics. I had to understand patriarchy, but understanding it didn't answer all of the questions. I now have a sense that patriarchy isn't quite as big as it once was, in women's minds as well as in reality. Men are not as all-powerful as they once were, and sexism is not as immutable and copious. On the most material level, the 1970 Kate Millett statement that the "military, industry, technology, universities, science, political office, and finance—in short, every avenue of power within the society, including the coercive force of the police, is entirely in male hands" is no longer true. Women are currently 20 percent of the military, up from 2 percent when Millett wrote those words, and have at least made inroads in every other institution she lists, as well—12 percent of the Senate, nearly 20 percent of university presidents, and almost 60 percent of university students.

Feminism came into my life in an organized but also theoretical way in college, just as I was having to deal with co-ed living arrangements and no curfew. In other words, just as I was creating my own boundaries and beginning to confront my own desires. My college, Lawrence, introduced Gender Studies into its curriculum my sophomore year, and the course had what I've come to see as a typical impact on the campus. Suddenly many young women (and a few men) were exposed to the passionate writings of the second wave—in other words, to women whose consciousness had been raised by radical feminist groups *and* who had, not coincidentally, grown up (and attended college) in a much more restrictive time for women. For many of them, getting an MRS. degree was the too-true expectation of their college careers. For my cohorts, we knew we'd have jobs, even if many of us still hoped to get married.

Gender Studies—particularly the work of Andrea Dworkin, Susan Brownmiller, Audre Lorde, and bell hooks—electrified my group of friends and other women on campus. It gave us energy, courage, and the impetus to interrupt some of the more offensive rituals on campus. I remember that there were mass defections from the three sororities after the first term of Gender Studies. The first feminist action I participated in was a protest of the Sig Ep house, which staged a charming annual "Rape-a-Theta" party. That action led to many others and to a whole new vocabulary such as *rape culture* and *date rape row* to refer to the string of fraternity houses in the quad.

The language and culture that feminism offered was instrumental in strengthening me as a person. I could see clearly what was off about a "Rape-a-Theta" event, even as I think I understood that the Sig Eps (one of whom was my boyfriend) weren't literally intending that as a mandate. What feminism—or, more accurately, the way I understood the feminist books I was reading—didn't help me with was maintaining my interpersonal strength with men. I had a way to "be strong"—I'd say, "I'm a feminist, that's sexist, I don't need you or marriage!"—but I had my real feelings about men, which were more complex. In bed, I was terrified of being exposed as inexperienced, completely terrified to look at or relate to a penis. (What if I held it wrong?) Besides, calling out sexist behavior or being more commanding didn't make my college lover Brady more likely to commit to me. And it certainly made it almost impossible for me to admit I really wanted him. Researchers have discovered that "stereotype threat," that is, the mere presence of a preferred group (white or male) diminishes the performance of an unpreferred group. "You can extend the thinking to individual interactions," says Naomi Weisstein, the seventies feminist who is also a neuroscientist. "The presence of the male (preferred by society) can lower women's ability to strut our stuff." Pondering Naomi's words, I think of my reactions to men who hit on me in college—it was as if I had been bitten by a paralyzing viper that renders its victims insipid. I'd stand there at a frat party, keg cup in hand, listening patiently to this guy we ended up nicknaming "the monger," as he coerced me to dance. Rather than just look him in the eye, smile, and say, "No. Thanks, I'd rather not grind to this Bob Seger song," I'd create an elaborate reason why I couldn't and then spend the rest of the night avoiding him. Curiously, I also felt a bit let down whenever any of these suitors lost interest in me. I couldn't be vulnerable, and I couldn't be intimate. I'm not assuming that Brady and the mongers were any more evolved than I was, but I look back and am shocked by the fear of appearing needy that animated my interactions with men. Dodging that fear is probably why I mourned the loss of unwelcome suitors. At least they had been the needy ones, not me.

As Carolyn Heilbrun puts it in *Writing a Woman's Life*, "For a short time, during courtship, the illusion is maintained that women, by withholding themselves, are central . . . And courtship itself is, as often as not, an illusion: that is, the woman must entrap the man to ensure herself a center for her life. The rest is aging and regret."[28] In that dismal view, being with a man after you've learned you *could* be with a woman—*could* be with someone where there is no script and "nothing at all is given," as Zane IndiAnna (Alix Kates Shulman's heroine in *Burning Questions*) learns—is, well, slipping, and dangerously, toward a self-produced secondary role in one's own life. *Perhaps you aren't serious about revolution or even your own work ambitions*, goes the little voice in one's head. Slipping, not just because you might be relinquishing your only way of remaining central to your own life, but also slipping because of the rapidly developing, plausible-sounding theories of female superiority.

The most persistent feeling that feminist women who looked both ways had when they thought of men was that they were reverting to old, unhealthy behaviors. When I wrote in chapter 1 of my despair over my relationship with Steven, I referred to how quickly I became a doormat to his moods. At first, I believe he saw the "me" I am at my strongest and healthiest. We both did. But at a certain point—and it was slow and subtle, I can't put my finger on when—he took me for granted. The attention and respect I got from Amy Ray reminded me of who I was, and I came back to him with that backbone and had the best months of our relationship. My affair with her was, in a sense, self-preserving, and it was one of the many reasons I chose her, despite the love renaissance Steven and I wound up experiencing. I think of that maneuver as triangulating, using each relationship to shore up the other one. "Do two men make a

whole?" asked Erica Jong's Isadora Wing in one of my favorite novels, *Fear of Flying*. The only time Isadora gets the
love she wants from her husband is when she is cheating on
him with another man.

"So much of feminism is indigestible," Katha Pollitt said
to me once. She was referring to the fact that feminists won
so many quick, profound victories there for a few years, and
yet many of "the underlying structures of male privilege
have proved surprisingly resilient."[29] Pollitt has written essays in *The New Yorker* about her years in a passionate relationship with a serial philanderer, who commanded the
larger study in their apartment yet produced a fraction of
the writing Pollitt did. Avowedly straight, Pollitt didn't turn
to her own sex, but many of the women I interviewed did.
Especially when it comes to men, it's hard to live in a way
that coheres with what one believes. Melissa Dessereau, age
thirty-six, told me about her first dip into same-sex love, after which she felt relief that she could ditch men.

> At the time I really wanted to identify as a lesbian. Why?
> Well, part of me was fed up with guys, and it seemed to
> me like—I'm stammering because it sounds so ridiculous
> to make these blanket statements—I felt that I wasn't
> getting enough emotional connection in my relation-
> ships with men and I wasn't being seen or heard. I was al-
> ways rather easy, sexually. So, the relationships were set
> up to be very sexual with men. But even when I was in
> love and in relationships with boys or men, they weren't
> serious . . . they weren't enough.
>
> I didn't feel a lot of intimacy in sex with men and I felt
> more intimacy in sex with women, actually. I often felt
> like when I would have sex with guys I would become
> easily attached to them, and that wasn't necessarily being
> reciprocated. That was repeatedly happening, and I was
> kind of fed up with it.

One of the pleasures of the opposite sex is directly opposed to the intimacy—the being seen and heard—that the women I interviewed (and I) want. It's the fact of our mysteriousness to them and theirs to us that fires some of the relationship. As Ani DiFranco said earlier, "There was the game of men and women that I learned to play very young, almost as a child." Many of the women in this book spoke of the terror they felt dating a woman who could "see through the games," in Shulman's phrase, and "feeling really seen, like I can't pretend," in Ani DiFranco's words. When I found Anastasia, I think men had been alluring, especially as far as attention, but disappointing. I felt disappointed by Steven's often lackluster devotion to me and betrayed by another's unwillingness to be a partner. Most of all, I think, I was disappointed in who I became while with them. I often feared, with both men, that my friends saw me as a brittle, self-conscious wife, one who was worried that my man was either easily offended or being overly offensive. Moreover, I'm surrounded by other (seemingly strong, together) women who spend their days apologizing or translating or covering for inept or obnoxious male partners. "Oh, what Paul *meant* was . . ." I know how hard it is to access the friend behind the bad relationship. My friend Christine describes it not as awkwardness over meeting the boyfriend, but as extreme oddness in meeting a friend when she's with the boyfriend and she's unrecognizable. Seeing friends—usually strong, wonderful women—with shitty guys . . . well, it's enough to make you disdain men.

But in order to really choose women, as a bisexual or a lesbian, I can't just run from men into the default category—gay. I can't feel that I'm there in the relationship because, in the words of Bridget Jones's mum, I'm not trying hard enough. What, then, powers the compulsion to be with men? In part, of course, it's that it's the norm—a convention that makes it appealing or valuable, like writing for *The New York Times* (read by millions) rather than *Ms.* (read by thousands). Perhaps the fact that men emanate strength—power women have but don't often express—that far from the screw-up boyfriend emphasizing our damage, it's the soft, needy women who remind us of our own neediness.

Ani DiFranco's ever-evolving relationship with her female fans tells that story. To have them panting and nervous to see her repelled her. Men didn't act that way, and so she found herself drawn to men. It wasn't until years later—and after her divorce—that she realized "how much of myself those girls had given me." In their eyes, she saw a heroine, and so she became one, though she always knew better. "I'm no heroine," she sings in one song: "I just write about / what I should have done / I just sing / what I wish I could say and hope somewhere / some woman hears my music / and it helps her through her day." For men, she didn't need to be a heroine to help them through their day. Women reminded her of neediness and weakness; men did not. And the dynamic between her relationships with women and those with men gave her back herself.

When feminists thirty years ago began holding up their personal relationships to the scrutiny of their raised consciousness, mothers became the focus of countless books: from *My Mother, Myself* to *Mommie Dearest*. It wasn't until I began dating Anastasia that I realized how often I shut my father out of my personal life. It was as if it was unseemly or too Oedipal and sexual to involve him in my real problems or passions. I didn't have the insight even to acknowledge, much less challenge, my restricted relationship with my dad until I had the lens of bisexuality. As I've mentioned, when I first kissed a girl, I told my parents about it immediately. Or, rather, I told my mom, expecting it would trickle down to my father through our usual information-osmosis system:

Tell Mom big news, she tells Dad. My parents, both pro-
fessedly pro–gay rights, had to deal with applying their politics to their personal lives, and some latent homophobia
and confusion were bound to squeak out. Although Mom's
Elton John concerns weirded me out slightly, I trusted her
and her candor. I knew she would "get it" eventually and become the mom in Fargo that everyone could turn to for
non-hysterical advice about their queer kids. She loves to
be the hip matriarch.

My dad was a different story. I felt a coldness creep in. I
had no way of really talking to him about this new sexual
development because we didn't really talk about "personal"
things. Like sex—I called my mom when I lost my virginity,
not my dad. Or breakups—I go to Mom. I talk to him about
menstrual cramps and birth control, but only because I consider those issues medical and I want to make use of his doctor status to get free pharmaceuticals. Suddenly, in the wake
of my bisexual bombshell, I realized that my relationship
with my friendly, handsome, stable dad was nearly devoid
of direct communication. We loved each other, but there
wasn't intimacy. In a sense, there was no adult interaction.
Back when I began dating Anastasia, I was feeling vulnerable and paranoid. By Father's Day 1994, I had worked up a
certain pitch of resentment over the fact that my father
hadn't talked to me about my new girlfriend. I could tell he
was embarrassed about having a bisexual daughter. Using
our patented osmotic technique, I told Mom about my
growing dismay. She leached back the news that he wanted
badly to talk to me about this.

So, on Father's Day 1994, I called him. He jumped right
in, "Your mom tells me you think I am upset about your sexuality . . ."

"Yeah," I said, launching in myself, "I can see where you
might be self-conscious or uncomfortable because we'll now
be seen as a family that isn't 'normal' and straight and—"

"I'm not uncomfortable," he interjected. "I want you to be happy. It doesn't bother me one bit if you're gay."

Gay. I almost said, *"Hey*, who said anything about being gay!" but stopped myself. Although I do use the word *bisexual* to identify myself, not because it's more palatable, but because it's more accurate, my reaction that day belied more than a little internalized homophobia in me. The point of that conversation is that, for the first time, we talked about something I assumed *he* didn't want to talk about—given that all of my nitty-gritty life, love, and sex conversations were always among women at my house. We acknowledged the fact that he is left out of the loop (and chooses to opt out) in ways that might seem easier but that do diminish our ability to be close.

I still sense less willingness from my father to be frank with me. There is a politeness—a chivalry—that reminds me of boyfriends during the early days of a relationship, when they are courting. This chivalrous attitude is so pleasurable, I almost allow myself to forget that it often covers our more complicated feelings about our relationship, or my choices, or his own life. I can't legislate that my father be on truth patrol with me. However, by pushing forward when I feel afraid to interrupt our mutual admiration society with a fear or a burning question, I have unmasked his special "paternal" power somewhat.

When I've said that criticizing patriarchy is inadequate for describing male-female dynamics, it is in part because the world has changed since those second-wave texts were written (even *because* they were written). Still, constantly pointing out the oppressive and huge nature of patriarchy almost fetishizes male power, making it loom larger than it is. My need to see positive examples of female power is perhaps why I was so moved by the television show *Buffy the Vampire Slayer.* Here is a young woman who is incredibly powerful and yet she's a very real girl—relatable, vulnerable, and even tragic in a way that I associate with real-life feminist superheroes. In a sense, *Buffy* is more feminist than any book I've ever read, because she's not a critique, she's an actualization of feminism. In season 7 (the final season), Buffy confronts a vampire who, in life, was a slightly nerdy guy from her high school whom she barely remembered. As they exchange body blows, he draws her out about her life—he's surprisingly insightful—and tries to pinpoint why her love relationships never work. They rule out that she's scared of commitment and he gets her to acknowledge that the men with whom she is involved do love her. So what's the problem? "Is it possible," the vampire finally asks, "even a little bit, that the reason you have trouble connecting to guys is that you think maybe they're not worth it? Maybe you think you're better than them."

Buffy does, in fact, feel that she is better than the men in her life. Her father is absent, long ago opting out of the after-divorce visits. Meanwhile, in what we assume men have more of—raw strength—Buffy is indisputably better endowed. She has the martial arts skills of Michelle Yeoh, the fist strength of ten Mike Tysons. She is competent—able to come up with a plan and execute it—and she needs to be. Saving the world (and her loved ones) from horrifying danger is her everyday life. She's a feminist martyr, in fact, a third-wave version of Gloria Steinem (who can never rest, or *Ms.* magazine and ten other organizations will go under) or Alice Walker (whose commitment to world-changing art means that even those closest to her can't have any demands). When it all depends on you, and you alone, how can you have a relationship? You are always sacrificing yourself for something much larger.

The isolation born of being both so unique and so strong causes Buffy to repress feelings of vulnerability—and to feel paradoxically damaged. Her damaged insides are met by being involved with Spike, a vampire who understands her. He expresses outwardly the complex ugliness and fear she feels (so when they are together there is a reprieve from the loneliness), but she could never respect someone like him. She's trapped—so powerful, but unable to be with anyone. By realizing her own strength as a woman, she has effectively made herself undateable. She has to be alone. The plot echoes a real fear for confident, self-actualized women—will I be able to find love? Bonnie Raitt gave advice to aspiring women musicians at the 2005 Rockgrl Conference, saying, "You have to find an alpha who doesn't need to prove it." Maureen Dowd lamented her own dating life in her book *Are Men Necessary?*, quipping that she came from Irish servant stock and would have had a better chance finding a man by remaining in the servants' quarters than becoming a high-powered columnist for *The New York Times*.

Then there are the strong, seemingly together women with bad boyfriends. Like Buffy, do we feminist women turn to mediocre men who can express messiness so that we don't have to? Does it make us feel stronger, more powerful, or more competent by comparison—but also keep us measuring our worth in relation to others rather than to ourselves? The strong woman/bad boyfriend phenomenon reminds me of how I felt when I first began interacting with transgendered (male-to-female) women at book signings. The women whom Amy Richards and I met during the *Manifesta* tour often came with a critique that the book had no discussion of transgender rights. I felt terrifically defensive—obsessed with the way the M-to-F pre-op women would dominate the evening, often with just their physical bigness. I hated the way they invaded a woman-only space, seeming to merely endure our reading so they could get to "their" part of the evening. "They wouldn't—couldn't—do that if they had been born women," I seethed. "You don't see

female-to-male pre-operative men heading to the Harvard
Club to demand inclusion. Why is it always women who
have to make more space and take in everything?" But as I
learned more about the history of transgenderism and met
more transgendered people—M to F and F to M and points
beyond—I revised that interpretation. I wonder now if it offended me that these women could be aggressive and take
up space while I still thought I couldn't.

At the end, we don't know if Buffy can find the kind of
love that won't make her hate herself in the morning, or the
kind of man who needs her to pretend that she's weaker
than she is. I don't know if I will find the equal, supportive,
loving, romantic, hot relationship I imagine for myself, either. But the presence of a straight man like Joss Whedon—
the creator of *Buffy*—in the world is reassuring. He's the son
of a feminist mom and a dad who wrote for *The Dick Van
Dyke Show*, my idea of the perfect gene pool. He proves that
men have absorbed the riddles of modern feminism, too, especially when he dramatizes a line such as "Maybe you
think men aren't worth it."

The seven-year *Buffy* series is an important and accurate
allegory of what it means to be a feminist today. The second wave had *Sexual Politics* and *The Dialectic of Sex*, but I'll
take *Buffy* any day. Among the reasons is the fact that at the
end of the cycle, when we've experienced years of being
told that there can be only one slayer—that her life is important but short and violent and without a certain kind of
love or happiness, that this has been foretold—that all
changes. The final episode depicts Buffy asking new burning questions: Who says there could be only one slayer?
Who says she has to die before another girl can meet her
potential? She and her powerful (bisexual) Wiccan friend
Willow devise a way to distribute Buffy's power. The final
scenes show girls standing up to abusive fathers and hitting
home runs. It's all like a Nike-commercial, but it absolutely

powers my dreams of a feminist future—one where a woman doesn't have to be "the one" to be powerful, and where no one needs to hand off her strength in order for another woman to feel her own.

My next relationship after Amy was with a man, the aforementioned Gordon, and although we also didn't work out, for lots of reasons, at first it seemed that I had evaded that paralyzing feeling I'd always had with a man. I was certainly more confident during sex—or, to be more accurate, willing to cop to a certain lack of finesse. My vulnerability was returned by Gordon, and for the first time in my life, I had a friendly relationship with a penis. I had changed enough—gained enough confidence—and therefore expected things I never had before. Gordon also went to Seneca Falls with me and to the Matilda Joslyn Gage House, two locales to which I didn't have success bringing other men I've dated. At the end of the day, I like men and want to have them in my life, whether or not I sleep with them.

In her introduction to the 1974 book *The Bisexuals*, Barbara Seaman wrote, "The women in this book complain that most men are insensitive or selfish lovers with whom they cannot communicate." She is describing women already in the throes of a feminist awakening, who use bisexuality to have better sex lives. Seaman cautions the reader, though, to note, "As you read this book, ask yourself the following question: How many of these women tried to openly state their complaints to their male lovers?"

In *Fire with Fire: The New Female Power and How to Use It*, Naomi Wolf calls for a radical heterosexuality—a world in which men both cook and cry and women do their fair share of programming the VCR. When this book came out in 1993, Anastasia and I laughed wickedly at many of Wolf's claims, especially the one where she says that she's seen the word *love* trigger an erection. "Me, too," Anastasia or I would shriek, "as in 'I'd love to give you a blow job'!" In order for us to grow as individual women, men had to be two-dimensional idiots. We were better off not publicly failing in our attempts to create better relationships. I look back and I think: we were really scared to take ourselves and our needs seriously when it came to men—but bisexual women need to learn to do just that before they can assess whether or not men are, indeed, worth it.

CHAPTER 8

SEXUAL TENSION: BISEXUAL WOMEN AND LESBIANS

Some lesbians are afraid of bisexual women because they don't want to compete with a man for a woman's attention. They might also believe if they had sex with you, they'd have to do all of the work. But there's no excuse for bi-phobia.

—Patrick Califia, once the lesbian Pat Califia, from his sex column in *Girlfriends* magazine, June 2003

In early January 2005, I was finishing up producing a film chronicling women's abortion stories. At the editor's house one day, we screened a rough version for a young filmmaker named Suzie, who had just completed a documentary about the war in Iraq. The day was snowy, and I had galumphed over in sopping wet boots, sliding along the sidewalks with three-month-old Skuli in his sling. The minute the door opened, Suzie helped me out of my coat. She also held Skuli like an old pro while I wriggled out of his sling, gamely entertaining him as if I were a long-lost friend rather than someone she'd met only thirty seconds earlier. After the screening, as we went over her notes, she was subtly cognizant of my son, playing with him in the millisecond before he was about to scream, cutting off any tantrums before they could erupt. In effect, she was also subtly cognizant of me, as the mother who would have to be responsible for Skuli alone if she weren't being so sensitive.

Suzie was clearly a lesbian. I knew before she said anything, and before we exchanged "Are you gay? I'm gay" embroidered conversation. (My embroidery? I always drop the phrase "my ex-girlfriend.") Months later I told our mutual friend, Natasha—who had brought Suzie in to critique the film—that Suzie was my type. "She's *my* type, too," said the now-married Natasha. "In fact, she's my ex-girlfriend." When I ran into Suzie at a screening months later, I blushed. *She's definitely my type*, I thought. I discussed this blush with my friend Gillian, the director of the film, and she didn't get Suzie's allure. "I just don't see what you and Natasha bonded over." Hmm, what was it? Suzie was not a glamorous, naughty, tomboy lesbian like Shane on *The L Word*. Nor was she a beautiful Portia de Rossi type. She was simply sort of butch and gallant like a guy, and good at child care like a girl. She made me feel taken care of in a way that goes beyond what a friend can do for you and seemingly beyond what I have ever been able to expect from a boyfriend.

Dating Amy was the first time I was in love with a lesbian—that is, an "out," actualized, five-star chica. Add to this the fact that Amy is also a famous lesbian, even an icon of queer pride and honest living, and you'll sense why my relationship with her gave me ample opportunity to contemplate what it is to be with a woman. I was both immediately read as queer and (often) blissfully free of covert homophobia, since many people wanted to meet her, just as many otherwise racist people want to meet Michael Jordan. Fame has its own ability to build bridges. With Anastasia there was always the opportunity, which I often took, to be mistaken for straight—maybe we were "just friends." We were both new to queer love and attraction and vacillated between making out publicly and competing for the attentions of Traver, a nephew of the owner of *Ms.*, who looked like a petite J.Crew model and worked down the hall. I was younger with Anastasia and prone to doing more cringe-inducing things: drunkenly making out with strangers at a bar or taking off my top and dancing around in a black lace bra at an Ani DiFranco concert. At the time of this latter smooth move, I didn't know whose attention I was trying to get, Ani's or that of the guys in the audience. By the time I met Amy, though, not only was I with a person who knew who *she* was, but *I* was also firmer in my identity. I understood by then that I had been trying to get Ani's attention (and failing), by using my (putative) sex appeal—something I did with guys.

Pre-bisexual awakening, I always resented how sexual attractiveness could be deployed by women in order to budge to the front of the line and get to a desirable person. Once I discovered feminism, I had theories of sisterhood and the male gaze to use against women who so shamelessly sought attention, to keep them in line, if possible. Aggressive flirting struck me as unfair, something that good women with feminist consciousness should be above doing. Because of my self-righteous exterior, I had to seek attention covertly ("I don't know why Lance is coming on to me! It's not my napkin-size dress, *I'm sure*") rather than overtly. The skimpy dress worked with my incoherent college feminist philosophy because we were big on promoting women wearing whatever they wanted, à la "My Short Skirt" in *The Vagina Monologues*. Phyllis Chesler addresses this in her book *Woman's Inhumanity to Woman*, in which she argues that a portion of the betrayal that some women feel about other women would be diffused if we simply acknowledged competition and aggressiveness as human qualities rather than male qualities. It took me a while to understand for myself that I could have personal ambitions and still care about all women moving forward, too.

Beginning with Anastasia, though, I began to move toward what I wanted more openly. She was hands down the office pet during her stint at *Ms.*, with everyone from the very cool lesbian executive editor to all the folks down the hall in Gloria Steinem's office adoring her eager smile and gorgeousness. Our affair meant I got to be closest to her. Greedily seeking women's attention and compliments didn't seem so . . . lame and unevolved. I remember a mix tape I made for her that had a drawing of two girls holding hands, under which I wrote "unavailable." It felt strong, as if we were retiring from that game.

In general, women who have looked both ways are an enormous part of the queer world—creating the community alongside the five-star lesbians who haven't ever fallen in love with guys. If you examine the strategies of the major gay organizations, they don't discriminate against bisexual people—in fact, they include B as part of their GLBT mandate. Bisexuals rate an initial, but there is no organizing around bisexuality. Lambda Legal Defense was founded in 1973 and has taken on thousands of cases; yet it has never had a single bisexual case on the docket. This is in distinct contrast with the recent and dramatic increase in cases involving transgender people—seven cases out of a thirty-case docket in 2005 alone. T was added to the mandate at the same time as B, but "bisexuals are simply invisible within the community," according to one Lambda staffer. "There is one conference each year that deals with bisexuality explicitly. For years we didn't even send anyone to it."

Despite the lack of overt bigotry, there is a tension (a lot of it sexual, thank goodness) between lesbian-identified women and women who look both ways. It mirrors some of the suspicion and resentment among different generations of feminists because it hinges on that nastiest of sins: entitlement.

This scenario is perhaps emblematic: at a panel I moderated at the November 2000 Rockrgrl Conference called "Out on Record," the conflict between self-identified bisexual women and lesbians was immediate. The panel—consisting of Luscious Jackson drummer Kate Schellenbach, singer-songwriter Melissa Ferrick, and women's music movement heroine June Millington—thus far had discussed coming out as public figures, the paradox of the lesbian or feminist audience (they're loyal but expect you to play for free), and how women-run venues often have bad sound systems. A singer-songwriter by the name of Edie raised her hand during the Q-and-A and told a personal story. The year before, she had been nominated for a GLAMA, the gay and lesbian version of a Grammy, mentioned earlier by Ani. Edie, who is bisexual, was dating a man at the time and she felt "as if [she] couldn't bring him to the awards ceremony," that he would be unwelcome and she would feel tacky and uncomfortable. So, just like Jodie Foster and Kevin Spacey at the Oscars, she brought her mom. "I guess I think it's not fair," said Edie, as audience members all but rolled their eyes.

Melissa Ferrick, who came out just after Melissa Etheridge did and received a good deal of mileage out of being "the other Melissa," finally snapped: "Look, I don't think you know what it feels like to be a lesbian. I *always* have to watch my back, Edie, and I don't think you can understand that when you do it part-time." Heads nodded all around.

Ferrick is right. Bisexual women don't know what it's like to be lesbian, if there are even universal elements of lesbian experience. I didn't have a crush on my gym teacher. I didn't insist my name was Billy and wear a blazer to kindergarten. We might not have been terrified to look around the locker room in high school because someone might think we're staring too hard. We don't *always* have to "watch our backs" when holding hands with a new love. And Ferrick doesn't know what it is like to be Edie, and feel like her relationship with a man negates her relationship to the queer music world. And Ferrick doesn't know what it's like to be me and have to constantly crowd every conversation with sign posts ("ex-girlfriend," "ex-boyfriend," "baby's father") to indicate the whole person I am.

For all of the wonderfulness, dating women has several discomforting elements of intimacy for me. Some have to do with the very similarities—the automatic empathy for what it is to be a woman—that make me feel turned on and reassured. I dislike my period even more when I'm involved with a woman, for instance, partly because there are two people's blood and crampiness and feeling unsexy to deal with and partly because it seems so . . . pointless. We aren't worried that one of us is pregnant, so there is no relief when I get it—it's just a nuisance, a nuisance that has no exoticism to it. My friend Barbara, herself a legally married lesbian in Northampton with two children, two cars, and two cats, once told me that she and her wife maintain total privacy around menstrual products and bathroom time. They call it "keeping the mystery." With Gordon and Steven, the mystery was there. There were so many close calls where I might have been pregnant. The phone call where I'd say, "Good news, I got my period," meant a sigh of relief that we'd share, but talking about my period felt risky and frisky. It was mine.

Perhaps it is this type of seemingly petty observation—this glib ability to choose between having to "keep the mystery" or not—that contributes to the antipathy between lesbians and bisexual women. The fact that I can like my period better when not with a woman sounds a little misogynist, and certainly heterosexist. For a long time I wouldn't allow myself to acknowledge those kinds of observations, because I hated that they implied any preference for hetero situations. (I also hate any evidence that I prefer homosexual situations. All of this is why, I suppose, I felt urgency to firm up a bisexual identity.) Women who look both ways challenge lesbians in that we mess up the carefully constructed community that is reinforced by persecution. We aren't always part of the beleaguered minority, therefore we take away some of the power of being oppressed. The Michigan Womyn's Music Festival typifies this kind of transaction. The beautiful—very seventies-feminist—culture they created occasionally slips into a new version of policing women. Ani DiFranco told me this story about a late-nineties gig she played at Michigan:

> I had put two female friends on the guest list. [My friends] got there before me. The festival workers wouldn't let them in even though they had passes and I had given their names. They kept my friend Shaun in this tent all afternoon and they wouldn't even give her any water. It was just really rude. Then, my friend MJ rolled up on her motorcycle with a Texas Tornadoes shirt on. It's a band—you know, buncha guys, Austin band. The Michigan women were like, "Take that shirt off or turn it around!" By this point I had to go to sound check, so I said to Shaun and MJ, "I'll meet you guys at catering," and I hear, "Don't use that malecentric language!" Me and my friends were just completely *manhandled* [laughs] that day. Later, I screeched out of those festival grounds in my little car, thinking, FUCK! This is what happens when this is the great ideal alternative community of safety and love and lack of hierarchy and power plays, because it was not like that at all. You know, it was experiences like that that told me that females don't have exclusive province over nurturing or energy or passivity and males don't have exclusive province over aggression.

Anyone who can access heterosexuality at some point is living a more socially privileged life than a lesbian is, as Ferrick's comment points out. This privilege gap hasn't stopped lesbians from dating bisexual women. In fact, some lesbians date only bi women; you could call it a sexual preference. And being a lesbian isn't automatically more evolved, but this occasional self-righteousness, or lesbian chauvinism, hasn't stopped bisexual women from being attracted to lesbians. Speaking of sexual preference, sleeping with men doesn't preclude one from claiming lesbianism. "If there is a definitive difference between lesbians and bisexuals," wrote Katie Hern in the January/February 1996 issue of *Curve*, "it certainly isn't whether or not you have sex with men." Hern was also commenting on the periodic rediscovery by the media of bisexuals. She cited a 1992 study of lesbians by sociologist Paula Rust that found that 43 percent of the lesbians she surveyed had had relationships with men since coming out. The numbers increased the longer the lesbian had been out; 91 percent of lesbians who had been out for twenty years or more had been involved sexually with men during that time. "In my experience," remarked an activist cited in the article, "there are way more women who call themselves lesbian who sleep with men than there are women who call themselves bisexual who do. And who gives a shit, anyway?" My own list substantiates the argument that sexual practices alone do not make the dyke: Norma McCorvey, a "lover of women," in her words, for most of her life, was also the pregnant woman who became Roe in *Roe v. Wade*; the very out director of the GLBT students groups at Dartmouth, who was also married for many years; Holly Near; Elizabeth Ziff—the list goes on.

Bisexuality, like feminism, has freedom at its root—the need to have more, not less, to say "and" not "or." Liza Featherstone, my former *Ms.* colleague, felt liberated to be feminine within a same-sex relationship, a liberty she didn't want to or didn't need to take with men.

I should say while I had had sex with other bi or straight-ish women, I have never had an actual relationship with

them. I've really had relationships with lesbians. I remember at some points with my last girlfriend when I
would think, "I would be happier with another bi woman
or a man." There are things that are so great about being
with a lesbian, but there are also things that are so strain-
ing. I'm not sure everyone would experience it that way.
Again these are huge generalizations, but they're based
on my experience. It sounds weird but you have more
freedom to express the range of your sexuality to a man
or to another bi woman. If my husband Doug and I go to
our neighborhood bar, which is Saint's, a queer bar near
Columbia, we can just check people out. And it's fine because men are in this privileged position where they all
think it's fine for women to be attracted to other women.
Lesbians aren't in that position. You cannot so easily go
somewhere with your girlfriend and observe that a guy is
really hot. You could certainly go places and observe
other women, and that's really great.

I asked Liza if her girlfriend took pride in having landed her.
"Yes, actually. My long-term girlfriend was particularly good
at expressing that. She was smug and she felt like she was
sort of one-upping men." Liza liked being an asset to her,
dressing up carefully if they were going out in order to
reflect positively on her girlfriend. "It's not something I
wouldn't do for a man, but not so consciously, and I wouldn't
feel so good about it!" Liza felt that it was more of a triumph
for a woman to have a trophy girlfriend, whereas with a
guy, it would simply be a cliché. "Unless, of course, I was
the trophy of a man who's a really big dork," Liza said, "so
no one would expect he could have you."

From feminist trophy chicks to getting props at the
GLAMA awards, being a lesbian has its privileges. Lakey,
the coolest of the Vassar clique in Mary McCarthy's 1963
novel *The Group*, is a lesbian. When the girls find this out at

the end of the book, they worry that she'll think that they are retrograde because they *aren't* lesbians. Candice Bergen portrays Lakey in the overwrought and poorly acted film adaptation—and her suave gorgeousness does make her hetero sisters appear a bit drab. Within mainstream culture, you could argue that the bisexual woman has more cachet, but in the gay world, in the alternative communities people have worked so hard to build, the bisexual woman is acceptable only when alone or with a girlfriend. A spate of early-nineties queer films underscore this: In *Go Fish*, when the butchest baby dyke in the film is revealed to be sleeping with men, too, she's surrounded by her lesbian friends, who shout nasty epithets. Even films meant for a more mainstream audience, such as *Chasing Amy*, portray coming out as bisexual to a gay community as potentially painful as coming out as queer to parents.

The story of Jan Clausen, who appears in chapter 3, is the epitome of the feared and cast-out (of the lesbian fold) bisexual. Her somewhat liberal family modeled the extreme division of gender roles in 1960s American middle-class life, where the mother was a servant to the entire family. Clausen identified with her father, "although I think I often accepted the idea that I would grow up and have some sort of female occupation." Clausen moved to New York City in 1973, at age twenty-three, when radical feminism had begun to lose momentum, but there was a well-established network of lesbian-feminist culture in the city, people creating a thriving margin to coexist with a mainstream poised for the backlash. Clausen found her way to a poetry collective in Brooklyn that included on its edges writers such as Audre Lorde, who once wrote a poem to Clausen. She soon developed a reputation as a big fish in that pond, and enjoyed an audience for her poetry created by lesbian-feminist activism. She lived with a fellow female writer for twelve years, helping to raise her lover's daughter (from a previous marriage).

> I've had many lesbian friends who were worried [then] about being "found out" as gay, but that wasn't my story. I had a teacher in junior high who I'm sure is a lesbian, with whom I had an intellectual, erotic relationship. Not a physical attraction at all, just a sort of luminosity in regards to the exchange of ideas and just feeling selected. At the same time there was also a boy. We were the two brainy kids and I was very attracted to him. I had this fantasy we just belonged together. Rather than gay, what I felt when I was in high school was that there was a choice between being a subject and being an object, and I knew I wanted to be a subject. I felt like a subject a lot of the time, too. I also thought there were people who assumed if you were a woman, you were an object. So how was I supposed to reconcile all of that? I tried to imagine myself into the subject position by having women as objects.
>
> There was the critique back then that lesbians were all man-haters, or had simply had a bad experience with a man, but negativity wasn't what drew me to women. There were so many positives to being with women. It really was a sense of the universe opening up, erotically and psychically. In every way, being with women helped me [self-actualize].

Clausen and her lover became a publishing power couple. Then, after a few years when the relationship (and feminism) was less hot and coherent, Clausen began doing international activist work. During a trip to Nicaragua, she fell in love with a man with whom she still lives. The divorce, in effect, from her partner included a brutal separation from her small but robust lesbian literary world. Suddenly she was afloat in a more mainstream-looking milieu: in love with a man and no longer connected to the ardent lesbian audience she'd previously written for.

When she and her partner split up, the divorce tore them apart emotionally, but also professionally. In practical terms, she knew she had lost some of her audience. "Internally, I lost my footing in a way," Clausen says. "I think I needed to break with a sense that I knew who I was writing for, and I needed to do a lot of groping." And she garnered public derision as a well-known lesbian feminist who had betrayed her peers. "I became like an inkblot test for people to project all their feelings about sexuality, or their own sense of ambiguity, or their fear of desertion by other women, their fear that they might be left *being the only one*."

Jan Clausen wrote a controversial essay in 1990 called "My Interesting Condition" for the now-defunct magazine *Out/Look*, where she described feeling cast out from her lesbian community when she fell for a man. The essay provoked a firestorm of intense opinion from women who identified as lesbian, such as this response from Lorna Hochstein, Ph.D.:

> I don't even know this woman, but I felt angry that she not only "switched allegiances," but had to be public about it. It felt embarrassing! . . . I know I am not alone in at least some of these feelings. But why? Why does it matter? Why am I angry, disappointed, [and] embarrassed by the actions of a woman I will never meet? Is it simply narrow-minded bigotry? Or is it lesbian politics again? Is it an easy willingness to trash another woman who has chosen to live her life differently from my own? Maybe it is. And yet, I believe there is more to it than that.
>
> In a world where all things were equal, I probably

wouldn't care about with whom Jan Clausen sleeps. In a world where no one judged, criticized, or devalued me because I love and have sex with a woman, I probably wouldn't care about [once lesbian-identified womyn's music star] Holly Near's romance with men. In a world where my choice to love a woman was as supported and valued as another woman's choice to love a man, I probably wouldn't care if any woman exchanged loving a woman for loving a man. But that's not the way the world is.[30]

I like Dr. Hochstein's raw response to once lesbian-identified women following their hearts toward men. I appreciate her pique that a woman such as Clausen not only fell for a man, but also wrote a tell-all book about it. And I accept her rationale for her anger: that because of homophobia's impact on Hochstein's own life, she can't applaud when one of her "allies" leaves their beautiful struggle to join the socially anointed and conventional world of being with men.

While I understand Hochstein's pain, I know on a cellular level that Jan Clausen isn't caving to convention, even when her desires fit in with convention. Clausen and other bisexual women have some privilege within the heterosexual paradigm. But, if there's one thing I've come to believe about privilege, it's this: the worst thing you can do with privilege—whether it's money, education, beauty, or connections—is deny it. The best you can do is use your privilege in the service of changing the world.

I am exactly twenty years younger than Jan Clausen. The year she came into New York City women's liberation, I was a three-year-old living in Ft. Lewis, an army base in Tacoma, Washington. Still, I have experienced some of what Clausen describes. When I began feeling attraction to women, I felt an amazing sense that the world was totally remakeable.

Part of the call of women was pure sex appeal and flirtation, but another part was the deliciousness of entering a world in which it seemed, in some obvious yet oblique way, that the decks were no longer stacked against me. I felt totally beautiful and less noticeably (to myself) threatened by other women and their looks. Why? I guess when men were in the picture, it often seemed as if the beauty critique was much more rigid—Amy Ray might not have rated as a ten. But within our feminist, woman-centric world, Amy was a huge sex goddess. Over the years, I came to recognize some of the stalkers she attracted—beautiful Daryl Hannah look-alikes, tiny punk rock girls, two-hundred-pound butch women in dickies, even one fan who dressed and styled her hair exactly like Ray's—all in lust with Amy. I liked that world. Not the stalkers, but the one where there were more varieties of beauty, not less.

I also related to the big-queer-fish-in-small-lesbian-pond aspect of Jan's story. The suddenness of getting the attention one craves for talent or attractiveness, or both. Melissa Ferrick cops to that, too—when she came out, she had a news hook and a new audience in one fell swoop. No longer one of thousands of young, white females trying to make it in rock 'n' roll, she was now one of a handful of gorgeous young lesbians making it. Thus, she became more singular, even if she was later dropped by her mainstream record label, Atlantic.

Most of all, though, I relate to Clausen's observation that after she left her gay marriage, many other women would confess their not-strictly-lesbian desires and lives to her, as if she were a priest for complex sexuality. About two years into my relationship with Amy Ray, I attended my ten-year high school reunion. Although Amy didn't attend the Ramada Inn soiree with me, many people knew that I had a girlfriend. Soon I found myself attracting everybody's one story of having gay feelings. It was kind of nice, in that I, too, harbor fears of being "the only one," as Clausen put it, but it was also rather odd. Around 1:00 a.m., as the gang of aging kids gathered in a hotel room to drink Schlitz and I decided to head home, a super-nice girl called Kathy asked me to have a cigarette with her in the lobby. She and I had been friends in junior high but had lost touch in high school when she hung out with orchestra geeks and burnouts. She had been worried about coming to the reunion because she had had "a relationship that none of [her] friends approved of." What was the problem, I asked her, drugs? Violence?

"Well, it was with a gal," she said and then proceeded to tell me about the woman she left her husband for and about the queer scene in Fargo. *Wait a minute*, I thought. There were people like that here?

"If people [call me] bisexual," Jan Clausen told me, "I don't say anything. It's certainly the nearest label for my sexuality in one word, and on that level, I don't really mind, but it seems something like an accommodation . . . an either-or, the third term to gay or straight, and I think it's sort of a cobbled-together category built out of pieces of the ideas of what gay and straight are. I think there's something wrong with the whole system." Indeed. Perhaps the whole system is screaming out for more flexibility. If Kate Millett said that *gay* was a term that straight America made up to deal with their own bisexuality, then maybe *bisexuality* is a term we use to deal with our own fear of sexual fluidity and the dynamic nature of attraction.

Amy wrote a very honest song that gets at the yearning she felt, too, to have the kinds of relationships she wanted with men. It wasn't often, but there were times when she wanted to relate to men and couldn't. She understood that it had to do with assumptions about her made by guys—that she was butch and gay, so what did she need or want from them, or that she was butch and gay and thus a competitor

for their privileges. But it also had to do with gaining acceptance in a more general way:

> *I can get the girls*
> *But the guys just laugh . . .*
> *So this is the measure of me*
> *Even though it shouldn't be*
> *The lion lays down with the lamb*
> *I can't do it so I ain't worth a damn*

To me, that song points to a truth that mere pride, as crucial as it is, or mere visibility, as key as it is, doesn't touch:
acceptance. For all women, that means understanding how
devalued women are—that the fascination with men or the
power they have to bestow legitimacy on a relationship, no
matter how lame or dissatisfying the relationship is, is cul-
turally imposed. In order for a bisexual woman to truly believe she is choosing another woman, she has to figure out
her relationship with men.

So, though common today, bi "dalliances" are presumed
to be trendy and contrived, manipulative and false. The
more legitimate political sexuality described by second-
wave feminists embraced same-sex love between formerly
straight sisters, but only when rendered as a conscious
choice to eschew the patriarchy altogether. The rhetoric of
the self-described lesbian (or the one who isn't looking both
ways) hints at distrust that bi women are confused users.
The musician Meshell Ndegeocello included a song in her
album *Bitter* in which she laments that her bisexual lover
doesn't know why she is with a woman. Ndegeocello implies it is orgasms and says, "You can teach your boy to do
that." Meanwhile, the opposite is true: If it is just sex, then
why deal with men when lesbians are so great at giving orgasms? According to the lesbian comedian Marga Gomez, if

women are going to be attracted to men, it better be because Marga can't deliver.

> I have this friend, let's call her Absinthe; she's hot and tests my empathy daily with her man-love talk. We're at a Johnny Depp movie and she whispers, "His hands are exquisite." Not the first time I've heard this from a woman who left women for men. Apparently it's hands they're after. Hey, ladies—I got hands. They are exquisite and highly trained from years of fingering and fisting. My hands can kick your new boyfriend's hands' ass. All I'm saying is go for something a lesbian can't give you, like testicles or musk or unwanted pregnancy. Don't be bragging about how your man cries or listens to you. You can get that with us.

My friend Kristen used to joke that lesbians aren't man haters—they have no reason to be. It's women who sleep with guys who have rage percolating in their veins toward men. This lesbians vs. straight women mentality misses the mark, though. In my lesbian world, I had privilege; one of the most intense privileges was being with women within the "Eden built by Eves" that feminists have created (from the Michigan Womyn's Music Festival to women's bookstores). And yet, I couldn't help but notice even then that in most areas of daily life, you deal with men, and there is power in learning how to be aligned with men. An obvious alliance with men is something that bisexual women have that lesbian women may want or need. The desire to overstate male oppression (or laughingly leave the work to straight girls) can, in fact, be a way of opting out from thorny sexual politics, and opting out means the sexism we decry may not change—we just don't have to look at it.

CHAPTER 9

ON BEING ENTITLED: BISEXUAL POLITICS

No matter where I looked, I saw women oppressed by their sexuality. Feminists wrote about it all of the time—like in Bust *and even in mainstream women's magazines—but I kept wondering, where is the action on this? Where is the activism? How can we move it beyond the theories and into a practice?*

—Emily Kramer, describing why she wanted to start *Cake*, a series of events dedicated to straight female sexual culture

My friend Sara Jane Stoner attended the school I use as a stand-in for "bisexual incubator," also known as Smith College. She graduated in 2002, and while she was there, only about five people were members of the LGBT group on campus. "We were all so comfortable being queer there," she recalls, "we thought, 'why join a group?'"

It's the paradox of persecution—so bad for the individual, but so good for building community. As women and gay people gain more rights, the activist solutions to their problems fall more squarely on their shoulders, as individuals rather than as a movement. This isn't merely because they are "stronger" due to the gains of their social justice movements. It's also—and more important—because they are allowed to be complex individuals and not one big mass of people with the same needs and values.

There are many signs that the movement for gay rights is changing. One is in the variety of histories reflected in the "queer experience." In the same way that I didn't recall "losing my voice" at age ten (as *Reviving Ophelia* would have it), I don't relate to the gay catchphrase "coming out of the closet." I reject its implication that I have been harboring a shameful secret or have forced a part of myself to fester alone in a dark, windowless space. Coming out to friends and family for some is a sit-down conversation it takes years to steel oneself for, followed by tears, recriminations, and fallout. Other times it's as simple as referring to your girl-friend in casual conversation with a friend who just gets it. She gets it, because she has either had feelings for women herself or knows many women who have. These feelings and experiences are part of the culture, even while homo-phobia is still part of it, too.

When I first wrote the proposal for this book, queer pop culture wasn't the mainstream onslaught it is today. *Queer Eye for the Straight Guy* did not exist, nor did *The L Word*. Bush had just become president. Ellen did not have a great new talk show that proved how popular she was despite being gay. San Francisco's mayor Gavin Newsom hadn't yet rushed gay marriage out of the land of theory and into the messy world. The 2004 election—ushering in eleven anti–gay marriage initiatives—hadn't occurred. The Supreme Court hadn't yet decreed that consensual sex between two men (or, by extension, two women) doesn't warrant an ar-rest. In short, these last few years have marked unprece-dented strides for gay people's rights—to have families, to live as visibly as straight people—since even the opposition is progress. All of the news stories about gay marriage, for instance, make people who wouldn't normally talk about gay people or rights talk about them. I have to believe that it leads to the next steps of liberation, the ones where gay people aren't merely a cute cultural topic or fad to exploit. Even the famous Christian evangelist Billy Graham refuses to knock down same-sex marriage publicly. "I don't give ad-vice," he said during a visit to New York City on his 2005 tour. "I'm going to stay off of these hot-button issues."[31] Amen.

Although there were many awkward moments describing whom I was dating, I never *really* felt as if I had to hide my sexuality. For me, a more appropriate phrase may be that I came in rather than out, as in "came into my own"; or, as second-wave wonder Naomi Weisstein suggests, came into a movement; or even came into a new room I hadn't known existed, like that great dream we all have of finding a whole new wing in our house. I opened a door, but in other ways, I stepped off the curb, and into the traffic of rapidly shifting political realities and complicated emotional beliefs regarding gender, love, family, and sex.

One Christmas several years ago, I attended a showing of *The Talented Mr. Ripley* in Fargo. I thought the movie was tremendous. Matt Damon stars as a con man who essentially just wants to belong to the blond glamorous set typified by delectable Jude Law and graceful Gwyneth Paltrow. The film featured Damon back when he was still on the up-swing from *Good Will Hunting*, and all the kids in America wanted to ogle his thick neck and megawatt choppers. Since he and Ben Affleck were the hottest things this side of the Back Street Boys for the belly-shirt crowd, the theater was packed with pimply girls, not unlike the acned teen I once was.

Tucked into the stadium seating, our huge coats forming auroras around us of fake fur and nylon-covered goose down, sat my sister, my mother, my slightly butch girl-friend, Amy, and me. Tom Ripley, Matt Damon's character, is quite possibly gay—or, as it plays in the movie, bisexual—and he has several eyebrow-cocking moments with Jude Law in the bath. Later in the film, he gets it on with a Rupert Everett look-alike, although it's unclear if Mr. Ripley really wants this guy or is just using sex the way a hustler does. Either way, as the movie's suspense built, peeps were heard from the teen audience. Peeps that sounded like this: "OmiGAAAWD. He's gonna kiss him! I can't watch." "Oh

My *God!* Don't kiss him! Don't kiss him!!—*eeeeewwww!"* When we talked about it later, Amy characterized it as a combination, perhaps endemic to the age group, of giggling and disgust. "It was such a deep movie and yet people seemed so uncomfortable," she said. She was rather philosophical about it.

The girl's inane responses ruined the movie for me. I wanted to stand up and announce self-righteously, "If you can't handle Matt Damon kissing another male actor, you should leave right now because it's part of the plot." Or, "Your boyfriend, Matt Damon, is clearly not a raging homophobe. Why don't you learn from him, you Claire's Boutique cows!" I didn't, though, and one of the reasons I didn't was that I was there with Amy, and I felt vulnerable and *gay.* I am not the advocate who screams, "This is homophobia!" constantly. This is a strategic choice; I don't want to become or be perceived as a bitter harridan whom people stop inviting to their parties. In this case, though, my light touch was part temperament, part fear. What really disturbed me, a feeling I don't think Amy shared, is that I really believe (usually) that the world has changed for people who were once oppressed minorities. And yet, here I was at the West Acres Cineplex, surrounded by tittering fag-haters, impotently enraged. I realized in that moment that there is a lot of soul-depleting homophobia out there.

Amy decided that, in some ways, the teen girls gagging during the film made the movie better because there was real-life tension in the theater. We had to empathize with Matt Damon and his outcast character, so beautiful, so misunderstood, and so tragic. But it's the tragic part of being gay (or thereabouts) that I don't want any part of, honestly. It's not so much that I am afraid of it. It's more that tragedy is not the whole story and, like focusing on back-alley butchers to justify abortion rights, it's over-told. A few years back I visited a small college where the students excitedly recounted their plans for gay pride: "We're lining up a hundred white crosses on the quad to symbolize the hundreds and thousands of gay people who have been murdered over the years." *Yay—happy pride week. Here's your grave marker!* Which brings us to Anne Heche, who is neither pure nor tragic. She is sullied and easy to poke fun at—but she comes out on top. Many people with whom I've discussed Heche feel that she is overexposed (or just plain over), but I believe that her role in popular culture deserves a closer look.

I winced the first time I heard Anne Heche publicly refer to Ellen DeGeneres as her "wife." As I recall, it was about five minutes after they met, but what made me flinch was not how fast their relationship had moved (a cliché of both Hollywood love and lesbian romances), but the fact that Anne would use the term *wife* for her girlfriend/partner/lover. At the time, it reminded me of my childless-by-choice eighth grade Spanish teacher who always referred to her Pomeranian as her "daughter," or, more cloyingly, her "dogger." It struck me as desperate or delusional—why pretend that your dog, wonderful in its very own way, is a child? Why pretend your lesbian relationship that just began five minutes ago is the same as a marriage?

Despite my derisive snorts, I was excited to see Ellen coming out in a major TV story line and in real life. As psyched as I was to have a glamorous Ellen girlfriend to relate to, who flew in the face of lesbian stereotypes, Anne Heche appeared to be a bit of an operator. For instance, according to her 2002 memoir *Call Me Crazy*, she didn't recognize former boyfriend and ex–Fleetwood Mac guitarist Lindsey Buckingham as someone famous, claiming to have met him while playing a game she calls "Who's the cutest person in the airport?" They date for a while; then she gets together with Steve Martin, who she's similarly surprised to discover is profoundly famous. The only actor she's really familiar with is Harrison Ford, because she was allowed to see one movie as a child and it was *Star Wars.* Imagine her surprise when he just happens to be her costar fifteen years later in *Six Days, Seven Nights.* Heche claims not to have recognized Ellen DeGeneres the night that they met at the Vanity Fair Oscar party in 1997. "We inched our way through the crowd, [with a friend of Heche's] telling the who's who of it all until my eye settled on one particular woman in blue standing across the room. 'Who's she?' I asked . . . I couldn't take my eyes off of her. 'I want to meet her,' I said." Heche was "in luck"—her friend knew Ellen.

A couple of years later, Heche was married to and had a child with a cameraman who had worked on Ellen's HBO special, and I was even more curious—who was she before she stepped into pop cultural history?

I have been a fan of Anne Heche's acting since I was in high school and she was in her soap opera days—eighteen and plucked from her Chicago high school production of *Guys and Dolls* to become the twins Marley and Vicky on *Another World.* As Marley, the good one, Heche wore pale lipstick and Ann Taylor suits. Marley was long-suffering, with a breathy, mellifluous voice, and the pained eyes of a woman with a lot of responsibilities. I think she was a doctor or something. Vicky, the bad sister, was that same Heche in tight black catsuits, fetching hairstyles that I attempted to re-create, and either a glower or a seductive expression on her lips—nothing in between. Vicky was a wildcat in the Susan Lucci tradition—and was nominated for a Daytime Emmy along with Lucci in 1989. Both lost that year, but Heche eventually got one.

As envious as I was of her exciting career (I was, after all, still in my "I want to be in *Cats*" phase), it turns out Heche's life outside work was pretty awful. According to *Call Me Crazy,* there was sexual abuse from her born-again Christian dad, who also happened to be a closeted bisexual or gay man and was one of the first casualties of AIDS. Her Christian mother critiqued every pound Anne gained and refused to protect her from her dad—or even take her to the doctor when she had a suspicious diaper rash as a baby that Heche implies was an STD. Then there was the abject poverty and the fact that they weren't allowed to go to movies or watch TV.

But suffering alone does not a good story—or life—make, as the writers of *Another World* surely knew. They understood that Marley needed Vicky in order for the show to get the Emmy, just as any character requires foibles in order to be seen as human. In her memoir retelling of her life, Heche tries to be mostly Marley, the good girl who just wants people to love one another and doesn't ditch her lovers or scheme to succeed. But she has a Vicky side, too—the one who goes and gets what she wants, who's foiled but gets back up on that horse, the girl who flaunts her sex life and wouldn't be caught dead in Ann Taylor.

She pats herself on the back for standing by Ellen when the film *Volcano*, in which Heche costarred, came out. While I fully believe that Heche's PR staff was worried about how her new "wife" would play in Peoria, I think they probably also saw the lemonade represented by Ellen. In her book, Heche isn't necessarily comfortable or aware of what she really did in her relationship with Ellen. She can't, or won't, deal with the obvious—the fact that Ellen's fame and the circumstances (gay suddenly, coming out on national television) had a tremendous effect on Heche's profile. Her breakup couldn't be about leaving Ellen, the world's most beloved lesbian. In order to avoid that messy but human reality, she took ecstacy and claimed she had thought she was Jesus for several months. Heche will only consciously cop to the goodness she emanated by refusing to be closeted.

I think the Vicky/Marley dichotomy speaks to how "good," how Marley-esque, you have to be to be gay—or a woman. Ellen DeGeneres is, in a way, also trapped in that Marley mode. She is even less willing to speak of what transpired with Heche—another example of how self-identified lesbians contribute, unwittingly perhaps, to bisexual invisibility. Ellen took the high road, the one without the tell-all book. Other than a few wry comments, we don't know what Ellen thinks about Anne's public flailings. (Although Ellen did prove more recently with Portia de Rossi that dating straight-looking blond starlets is, if anything, her sexual orientation.) At this point in the evolution of gay rights, though, the high road is the route you must take because you have few options—you are responsible for being a credit to your queer race. The high road is, in this way, less evolved and liberated than Anne's messy example. (When I say evolved in this instance, I mean it lacks the gutsiness that feeds from privilege.) The high road trap happens for other communities and oppressed groups, those with so much to gain and so much to lose. You must be the *right* kind of heroine (black leader, gay politician, female democrat). Many second-wavers held women to this stultifying standard, and so did the suffragists.

Being half-straight, Heche could afford to take a variety of roads. And although Ellen's stature made her coming-out more of a big deal, Heche was the one pushing the gay rights agenda forward via public displays of affection. As Ellen told *The New York Times Magazine*, "A gay person would never have let me be so public because a gay person would know what would happen." Because Ellen was with crazy Anne, though, we didn't just have a coming-out episode of *Ellen*, we had wives holding hands on *Oprah*—in 1997! As Ellen later reported, she had never been affectionate in public with previous girlfriends:

> Anne went to grab my hand, we're walking down the street, she wanted to hold my hand and it made me feel

really uncomfortable, even though I'm about to make this huge announcement to the world that I'm gay. I didn't want to hold hands because people would look at me and it would make them uncomfortable and it would make me uncomfortable and I realized I still have a sense of shame about who I am. How am I supposed to say it's ok that I'm gay, but yet I still don't deserve the right to show affection in public the same way other people show affection?[32]

Heche is probably disingenuous about her innocent "Who's that!?" attraction to Ellen—there is no way that she could have been so unaware of celebrities given that she'd been an actress for years—but Ellen is afraid to own up, too. She won't interrupt the current narrative where Heche is actually straight and the relationship is thus invalidated, inauthentic, not love. In Ellen's public story, Anne is just a straight girl.

What Anne symbolizes to me is the great what-if—what if it were okay for *gay* people to have *straight* expectations? Not to "pass," or become palatable, or go back in the closet, but simply to expect what Heche took for granted: to not have to be careful and quiet about her love life. Heche's cluelessness and her sense of entitlement were annoying, but they were also her weapons against fear—fear of being gay in a homophobic society and in a very homophobic (though very gay) industry.

I phoned Heche in 2004 to interview her for this book. She was incredibly personable and called back right away to say that she'd love to talk when she was in New York that spring doing a play with Alec Baldwin. We spoke for a while about the premise of the book, about the fact that I wanted to demonstrate that because she was now married it didn't mean that her relationship with Ellen was inauthentic any more than any of her other relationships were invalidated by her current one. She seemed jazzed, even relieved, to have a venue that said just that.

When I called to schedule the interview, though, she had changed her mind. "I respect what you are doing," she said, "but I'm an entertainer—that's what I do best and that's what I want to be known for. My book says what I wanted to say on that topic." Her book doesn't say much about sexuality, but she does end it with this thought: "I hope you find happiness and love and peace because it is your right to have it."

While I would never insist that people who fall into the category that I describe as bisexual all use the word *bisexual* to identify themselves—in fact, I feel about eighty-five when I say that I'm writing a book about bisexuality, when all of the kids today say "queer"—it is at the same time a feminist act to firm up the existence of bisexuality. That doesn't mean pushing the term, but it does mean telling our stories—and taking them seriously, not treating our own lives as embarrassing or confusing. Jan Clausen echoes my suspicion that it's not making up new and better labels that we're going for here in our quest for liberation: "I think it would be about social expectations changing, not creating a new word. I can't explain who I am without telling my life story. Obviously, you're not going to do that in a lot of social situations but, ideally, I want to be able to expect the sense [from others] that erotic life is a lot more complicated than what that person is doing now. That what you see right now doesn't mean what they're destined to do or what they've been doing."

For those queer people who don't relate to the term, or the idea of a political movement based on bisexual identity, I say that we need to allow at least a little part of us to see the value of our complexity—bisexuality's potential in furthering the goals of feminism and gay rights. "Look, I'm not a lesbian," the activist poet June Jordan said to me with more than a touch of exasperation during a 1996 interview. She and sister poet (and former lover) Joy Harjo had just decided to withdraw their work from an anthology called *My Lover Is a Woman* because not all of their lovers were women. "As of 1991, I have identified as bisexual. I resent this huge resistance to complexity." June Jordan died in 2002 of breast cancer, but her succinct complaint still rings in my ears. For her generation, she was breaking ground—even breaking ranks—to publicly distinguish herself as bisexual (but still a feminist). At the same time that June and I were having this interview, though, high schools across the country were mobilizing their gay-straight alliances and demonstrating the changes wrought by thirty years of feminism and gay rights. Students, many straight-identified, fought their administrations and communities for the right to have gay clubs. Meanwhile, in dozens of towns, such as Salt Lake City, school boards decided they'd rather ban all clubs than allow a single queer organization. Those student activists will be the next generation of parents. To them, banning gay-straight alliances will be as bigoted as segregation. It's feminist to understand bisexuality as its own identity, too, because it's a chapter of women's history that has been suppressed and misunderstood, and one that has contributed substantially to current ideas about queerness. Naomi Weisstein, a second-waver who, though straight, has written some of the most perceptive analyses of what looking both ways means for women, says:

> The lesbian conversion in the women's liberation movement is one of the most stunning examples of the power of a collective, social movement to challenge our deepest notions of who we think we are and what we believe we can do. This chapter of our history should never be lost because it provides profound hope in our ability, through

collective action, to become what we want to become, and to mold our human society in ways that we would believe unthinkable before the transformation.

When I first started writing this book, I felt the title *Look Both Ways* referred both to an action—as in "look both ways before you . . ." cross the street or make any big decision—and to the aesthetics of lipstick lesbians, butches, and tomboyish straight girls. I saw the urge toward bisexuality as a means to figuring out how to have a satisfying, truly equal and truly intimate relationship, given an unequal culture in which we're still saddled with a consciousness that women are hardwired to do dishes, make less money, and repress our desires. I also thought the title reflected a burgeoning girlie movement within feminism and queer female circles. In addition to transgenderism's inroads into feminism (and vice versa), gay and feminist women were openly valuing traditionally feminine things, including the blond chick who wears a dress and waxes all her body hair off. This look was always overvalued in the mainstream more than butch looks, but it was devalued in feminist and gay circles. Of late, there is a movement dedicated to opening up access to looking however one wants within feminism, rather than seeing a look like that as fundamentally retrograde and exclusive of having a girlfriend or politics. Thus, I can look both ways (at men and at women) *and* I can look—appear—both ways, too, by not looking classically gay. Why be lipstick rather than tomboychick (besides, I suppose, having the preference)? It takes the edge off of a stereotype—allowing for women to take up a bit more space in the spectrum of fully human. I date women, but I don't signal to the rest of the world that I am part of a marginalized subculture. Or I date men, but I'm not a "typical girl."

The thing about being bisexual is that you don't really have to be out in the same ways. You can often pass for straight. This can be a weak situation politically—how can we organize people around gay human rights if we don't identify, and can't be identified by others, as gay? Very similar to the current situation of feminism—if we don't look like feminists and all agree that saving *Roe v. Wade* is our first priority, how can we organize as feminists? Given our diversity, the power in this case lies in our personal contribution to the world, not our contribution as part of a group moving as one and speaking in one voice. Our individuality is part of our power. In Vivian Gornick's essay about first-wave feminist foremother Elizabeth Cady Stanton, she makes the case for individualism—a peculiarly American value—and feminism:

> America had *not* been built on the bedrock of the family. In America, the ethos of self-creation had fostered a proud, prickly, adolescent inclination to retreat into what is often experienced as useful solitariness. In a country like Israel, such solitariness makes people go to pieces. But here's the paradox: that famous American loneliness, with its fierce credo of self-reliance, has, time and again, become a source of collective dissident strength.[33]

Because there is no single queer or straight experience, we have no choice but to exploit our individual strengths and stories for the betterment of gay rights and feminism. Bisexual women have a particular role in this struggle.

Bisexuality, as with girlie feminism, contains the liberating potential of aligning with a disparaged group but not being relegated—at least not full-time—to the ghetto. This is the political value of what is called, negatively, entitlement. The political weaknesses of entitlement (lack of consciousness) have been overstated—as with young feminists—and its potential for change has been neglected. Perhaps we need the privileged and clueless. We need those bridging people—those on the side of privilege willing to connect the gay and straight worlds—in order to get more done.

In the sixties, how much more slowly would the civil rights movement have moved without northern white students who presumed to know about racism? Black people had been organizing for decades, but the flood of rich white kids with a sense of entitlement also spurred freedom along, made emancipation visible, even when those white kids didn't always understand the costs and were gambling with more than their own lives. There are positive aspects to entitlement: *It takes someone who has known relative freedom, who expects it and loves it, to help ignite social change.* This is the person who has lost or might lose something and feels entitled enough to get it back.

The confidence engendered by a sense of entitlement has undeniable power, even without political consciousness. Mainly, that confidence adds to visibility. One reason gay people are discriminated against is because there aren't enough out *politicized* gay men and lesbians in positions of power—whether as elected officials, business owners, or even parents. I stress "politicized" because not all gay people fight for gay rights, just as not all women fight for women's rights. If people who've looked both ways become politicized on behalf of gay rights, it will become harder to discriminate against gay people.

Visibility is crucial to making bisexuality a political force, because it could take straight people from being the majority to being a minority. When we include bisexual women, our power to move gay and feminist rights forward lies in not just the 3 to 10 percent who identify as lesbian, but also the thousands and thousands of college students who are bi (the lesbians until graduation—LUGs—and the Ani fans). Power resides in the older women, such as the writer Joan K. Peters and Alix Kates Shulman and Alice Walker, who are now with men, but who have been in love with women, too—and whose lovers were critical to their feminist awakenings. In fact, in the case of Shulman, she may not have been able to value the man she lives with now (who shares little with the aggressive philanderers who characterized her early attractions), had she not fallen in love with women. Power comes to women who bring gay expectations to their heterosexual couplings. "It's hard to defeat an enemy that has outposts in your head," went an insightful slogan of the second wave (attributed to writer Sally Kempton), meaning that our internalized sexism is just as powerful as the concrete barriers thrown up by patriarchy. The experience of loving a woman and being able to be "oneself" with a man helps to defeat that misogynistic enemy within. By having romantic relationships with women, we learn how to be more confident and ambitious in sexist society—how to compete in the mainstream. Similarly, if male privileges—such as being the gazer rather than the gazed-at—are owned by bisexual (and gay) women as well as men, the exclusive power of the patriarchy begins to crumble.

During a visit home in June 2005, I picked up the *Fargo Forum* to encounter a front-page story entitled "Coming Out Stronger." A thirty-four-year-old "single" mother was profiled, as was a twenty-one-year-old student at North Dakota State University. The writer spent a total of fifty hours with the two, and penned two interesting portraits, notable in their normalcy as much as in their queerness. The reaction a few days later in the letters-to-the-editor section was dramatic. The first wave of letters decried the "sick, sick, sick" coverage; many letter-writers wondered why the daily lives of people who were gay could possibly be newsworthy. My father was dismayed by the reaction, the homophobia that appeared to be so rampant. But I saw another story: it's a certain kind of person who writes a letter to the editor, and they are often serial responders. Those homophobic letters, in turn, actually drew out letters reflecting the positive responses from quieter people who had enjoyed the *Forum* articles but hadn't thought to write in support of them.

This incident made the continuum of sexuality *and* homophobia clear to me, and how all of us are lurching toward *more* understanding and visibility of gay people, not less. The NDSU student who would not have been deemed newsworthy a few years ago—or who certainly would not have been written about in as positive a light—is the subject of a flattering and serious front-page story. The people who would have been distantly tolerant, such as my father, are allies; the people who once would have received roars of support for their position that homosexuality is "sick, sick, sick" are much more often a beleaguered minority.

The late and sorely lamented rock critic and feminist Ellen Willis introduces her 1991 collection of essays *Beginning to See the Light* by remarking how struck she is, now, going over all of this work she has created, by how much of her life has been concerned with freedom. She writes about sexual freedom, the freedom for women to have control over their bodies and thus their lives, the freedom implied by rock 'n' roll and the liberty of women to love the music and not just the guitar gods who make it.

When I take a look at my life—or at least at the years from thirteen to my current thirty-six—I marvel at how much of it has been committed to being included. I've tried to break down exclusion or get around it, even if it means looking exploitative or compromised. I'm thrilled that feminists critiqued Barbie and pointed out how unreal her figure is, but if they say I can't play with her, well then *screw them!* I don't want anyone to die in Iraq, but it's no more tragic or terrifying to me that a woman see combat than a man. Bisexuality walks similar terrain: I want to belong. I don't want there to be a space that I don't have access to.

For me, this fight for inclusion is linked to feminism. Inclusion is one of the reasons I am a feminist and one of the ways I define equality. Women have the right and responsibility to go where men go, be it to strip clubs, to war, to work, or to the bank. Men have those same rights and responsibilities with regard to women's spaces. When I apply this desire to trump exclusion to sexuality, it means that gay people deserve to get married and have kids and receive social approbation for their relationships, just like straight people. Moreover, straight people deserve what gay people tend to have: the privilege of equality in their relationships and freedom from rigid gender roles.

bell hooks writes convincingly of the margin as a space of radical openness, but a margin is still small, even if it's beautiful. It can't hold all of us, at least not for long. I know that women are transformed by the Michigan Women's Music Festival to this day. But unless women take the feeling they have at Michigan back into their regular lives and use the confidence to ask for more the other 359 days of the year, they aren't changing the world. That is why the utopian retreat of lesbian and feminist culture is a problem—it's safe, and by its very existence it perpetuates the mystical (untrue) power of heterosexuality, masculinity, and mainstream culture. It's not that I want the Michigan Womyn's Music Festival and Ms. magazine and Babeland (a sex toy shop owned and run by feminist women) to go away. I just don't want their value to be so solely and precariously based on the fact of being "other."

Freud said that love and work drive humans. That is true, but incomplete. We are driven by a need for connection, too, and, in some cases, those connections are most easily gotten through same-sex love. Some find it through heterosexual partnerships; others of us look to men and to women to meet our needs. I don't believe that bisexuality is more or less feminist than being straight or lesbian. I don't believe it is more queer than being gay. It's simply that people who look both ways deserve to a have a sexuality that originates in them, not one that's a reflection of who they are currently sleeping with. It is a sign of having rights in this society to enjoy the privilege of being subject, not object. As sexual beings, the struggle is to maintain or get to that subjectivity—to know who we are at all times, to have a core of sexuality that is our own.

"We have to stop bitching and become the thing we are preaching about," the musician Tori Amos says in Pratibha Parmar's film *The Righteous Babes*. Amos is not arguing that we actually want to become men, but that we have to allow ourselves what they have and not continue to congratulate ourselves for making do with less. Imagine standing at the top of a mountain and surveying the landscape with new perspective—instead of staying down in the forest, hardly able to see a few feet ahead. Looking both ways is not simply about behaviors—about sex or political actions. It's about consciousness. It is aiding some women to make a crucial step toward liberation. To know what it's like to be privileged (like a man) to behave, in a way, as we say men do. To see the spoils and think, "I can have this, too—I can have sex, a higher salary, objectification, control, love, what I want."

Feminism demands that we engage with men and with women. Moreover, the next decades of gay rights will be fueled by recognizing how common bisexual experience and love actually are. So much has changed since 1993 when I asked the interns if we were "all straight here." Back then I assumed that we *were* all straight, because nobody "seemed gay" to me. I also presumed that it was preferable to be straight, that we were all mildly fortunate to be heterosexual. Up until that moment, my point of view was that women-with-men was normal and women-with-women was alien, yet deserving of rights and respect. I hadn't examined those assumptions and hadn't even really tried to understand my own desires and hopes. I had the goals and expectations of feminism down, but wasn't sure how to get there from here. Since then, I have been on a journey to figure out what feminism means to me, not just what I have been told it is. One of the big lessons of that wonderful philosophy is that women aren't crazy or retrograde, but when their lives were described only by men, it appeared that they were both. Well, in a gay/straight world, my life doesn't make sense—many people's lives don't make sense unless we believe that sexuality is far more complex.

At thirty-six, I'm back on the curb, but I know enough to look both ways.

NOTES

1. William D. Mosher, Ph.D.; Anjani Chandrea, Ph.D.; and Ho Hones, Ph.D.; Division of Vital Statistics, *Sexual Behavior and Selected Health Measures: Men and Women 15–44 Years of Age, United States, 2002,* from *Advance Data 2005,* U.S. Department of Health and Human Services.

2. I learned this from *Odd Girls and Twilight Lovers: A History of Lesbian Life in Twentieth Century America,* by Lillian Faderman (New York: Penguin Books, 1991).

3. Marjorie Garber describes the various ways Freud perceives bisexuality in *Vice Versa* (New York: Simon & Schuster, 1995), p. 198.

4. *The State of the Workplace for LGBT Americans,* Human Rights Campaign, 2006.

5. Peter Gay, *Freud: A Life of Our Time* (New York: Norton, 1998).

6. Garber, *Vice Versa,* pp. 56–57, 101, 190–91.

7. Ibid., p. 181.

8. As quoted in ibid., p. 169.

9. Ibid., pp. 274–75.

10. Millett, quoted in her telegram-like memoir, *Flying* (New York: Simon & Schuster, 1990). I wouldn't have found this quote without first seeing it on page 2 of the anthology *Bi Any Other Name: Bisexual People Speak Out,* edited by Loraine Hutchins and Lani Ka'ahumanu (New York: Alyson Books, 1991).

11. As quoted in Garber, *Vice Versa*, p. 204.

12. Marilyn French, *Beyond Power: On Women, Men, and Morals* (New York: Ballantine Books, 1986), p. 519.

13. See Sabrina Margarita Alcantara-Tan's essay in *Young Wives' Tales: New Adventures in Love and Partnership* (Seattle: Seal Press, 2001).

14. The book doesn't say how Ivan Hill, the ethicist and professor who edited *The Bisexual Spouse*, came to that large number.

15. Again, Lillian Faderman's *Odd Girls and Twilight Lovers* is most instructive on this topic.

16. Faderman, *Odd Girls*, p. 63.

17. *Time*, December 14, 1970, p. 50.

18. From "A Fem's Feminist History," *The Feminist Memoir Project: Voices of Women's Liberation*, edited by Rachel Blau DuPlessis and Ann Snitow (New York: Three Rivers Press, 1998), pp. 138–41.

19. This expansive take on feminism's impact on sexuality was part of a letter Weisstein wrote in 1998 to *The Women's Review of Books*. The journal had just run a somewhat negative review of *The Feminist Memoir Project*, a book I found to be very illuminating but that the reviewer found to be insufficiently connected to lesbian rights.

20. Alix Kates Shulman, *Memoirs of an Ex-Prom Queen* (New York: Knopf, 1969), p. 266.

21. Alix Kates Shulman, *Burning Questions* (New York: Knopf, 1978), pp. 282–83.

22. According to a fund-raiser organized by the Olivia Records Collective in 1977 and documented in their liner notes to *Lesbian Concentrate*, in the three years previous there were more than one hundred custody cases involving lesbian moms who had lost their children to male exes.

23. Ruth Rosen, *The World Split Open* (New York: Viking, 2000), p. 254.

24. *Glamour*, April 2005, p. 128.

25. Bo Burlingham, "Don't Call Her an Entrepreneur," *Inc.*, September 2004.

26. Gay Lesbian Straight Education Network.

27. Anselma Dell'Olio, "The Sexual Revolution Wasn't Our War," *Ms.*, Spring 1972.

28. I am grateful to Anna Fels, whose fascinating 2004 book *Neces-*

sary Dreams: Ambition in Women's Changing Lives reacquainted me with Heilbrun's assessment of women's relationship to men.

29. From the afterword, cowritten by Katha Pollitt and me, to *Catching a Wave: Reclaiming Feminism for the 21st Century* (Boston: Northeastern University Press, 2003).

30. Lorna Hochstein, Ph.D., "When Lesbians Fall for Men," *Images* 9, no. 2 (Summer 1991), http://www.catholiclesbians.org/archives/fallformen.html.

31. *Newsweek*, "Perspectives," June 27, 2005, p. 23.

32. From an Ellen DeGeneres fan site, ellen-degeneres.com, which gives a blow-by-blow of her coming-out saga.

33. Vivian Gornick, *The Solitude of Self: Thinking About Elizabeth Cady Stanton* (New York: Farrar, Straus and Giroux, 2005), p. 129.